Dramatic Problem Solving

of related interest

Rebels with a Cause
Working with Adolescents Using Action Techniques
Mario Cossa
Foreword by Zerka T. Moreno
ISBN 978 1 84310 379 0
eISBN 978 1 84642 245 4

101 Things to Do on the Street
Games and Resources for Detached,
Outreach and Street-Based Youth Work
2nd edition
Vanessa Rogers
ISBN 978 1 84905 187 3
eISBN 978 0 85700 419 2

The Yellow Book of Games and Energizers
Playful Group Activities for Exploring Identity,
Community, Emotions and More!
Jayaraja and Erwin Tielemans
ISBN 978 1 84905 192 7
eISBN 978 0 85700 432 1

Performing New Lives
Prison Theatre
Jonathan Shailor
Foreword by Evelyn Ploumis-Devick
ISBN 978 1 84905 823 0
eISBN 978 0 85700 288 4

Once Upon a Group
A Guide to Running and Participating in Successful Groups
2nd edition
Maggie Kindred and Michael Kindred
ISBN 978 1 84905 166 8
eISBN 978 0 85700 380 5

Art in Action
Expressive Arts Therapy and Social Change
Ellen G. Levine and Stephen K. Levine
Foreword by Michelle LeBaron
ISBN 978 1 84905 820 9
eISBN 978 0 85700 270 9

Ritual Theatre
The Power of Dramatic Ritual in Personal Development Groups and Clinical
Practice
Edited by Claire Schrader
Foreword by James Roose-Evans
ISBN 978 1 84905 138 5
eISBN 978 0 85700 334 8

Dramatic Problem Solving

Drama-Based Group Exercises for Conflict Transformation

Steven T. Hawkins

Jessica Kingsley *Publishers*
London and Philadelphia

Permission has been kindly given from Boal's estate to include his exercises.

First published in 2012
by Jessica Kingsley Publishers
116 Pentonville Road
London N1 9JB, UK
and
400 Market Street, Suite 400
Philadelphia, PA 19106, USA

www.jkp.com

Library of Congress Cataloging in Publication Data
Hawkins, Steven T.
     Dramatic problem solving : drama-based group exercises for conflict transformation / Steven T. Hawkins.
    p. cm.
Includes bibliographical references and index.
ISBN 978-1-84905-325-9 (alk. paper)
1. Interpersonal conflict. 2. Conflict management. 3. Social psychology. I. Title.
HM1121.H395 2012
303.6'9--dc23

2012010751

British Library Cataloguing in Publication Data
A CIP catalogue record for this book is available from the British Library

ISBN 978 1 84905 325 9
eISBN 978 0 85700 667 7

Printed and bound in Great Britain

Contents

Preface

The formation of the Dramatic Problem Solving (DPS) process has been an interesting evolution. It really began when I was about five or six years old and my sister and aunt would be going off to audition or rehearse for the upcoming community theatre show. I, being a little brother, wanted to go along and see what all this was about. When I would get there, inevitably the director would need another player for a child's part and I was thrown onstage. This was my first acting experience and those memories of the excitement of the stage, the quiet that occurs in a theatre in the space between lines, the nervous energy, and the emotional high captivated me. Looking back now I see that I sensed the power of theatre for change even then. Later, when I was a teenager and went to Catholic school, I had a time of thinking I wanted to be a priest. I served as a sacristan daily at mass. This meant I got to lay out the robes for the priest, bring up the gifts to the altar, do the readings, and lead the call and response. It was a really good feeling to be up on the altar. Then, they told me the part about no girls and no sex, and well, it was so long to the idea of the priesthood. But, what had captured my attention was not the religion as much as the performance. The power of that audience, that silence, the ritual space. This is what I was drawn to.

So, logically, I pursued a career in education, because teachers are another group of people, like clergy, who get to perform on a daily basis and can count on a regular paycheck, which was different than what I saw my sister going through in her career as an actress. Education provided me a great chance to explore ways to weave drama into the classroom. For my master's thesis I did a research project on the impact of a play on the reading and self-esteem levels of students at a school for children with learning disabilities. Again, I was able to see the way that energy, that space could work as an agent for change; this time it was in the lives of my students.

While completing my doctoral course work in Conflict Analysis and Resolution at Nova Southeastern University I was still working in education. I decided to try to create a teaching tool that would demonstrate an application of conflict theory in an analysis of a particular conflict through the use of a dramatic presentation. I went about studying various theories of conflict and then writing a play about a conflict with characters within the play presenting theoretical analysis of the actions throughout. The play, entitled *The Corridor*, was a simple piece of dramaturgy. I sent it out for readings and advice from people interested in theatre for social change. Comments came back that the play was good but needed something more to be an agent of true change. Johnny Saldaña wrote to me and said that he wanted to hear more of the story of Maria, the young Mexican protagonist in the story. He wanted to know more about her, her life, her dreams, and her secret thoughts. It was then I realized that I didn't have that story inside of me, that I was not Maria and I could not say more about her condition. This was my ah-ha moment, my epiphany. I realized then that what I was trying to do was no more than a replication of the banking system of education that I had been brought up in. I was going to write and present this play and then facilitate dialogue so that everyone would understand better what I deemed important. What I was doing was leaving behind the people who were truly affected by the conflict. There was no praxis here, it was strictly theoretical and wasn't going to result in the change of anyone's lives.

This led me to question my practice and my own arrogance at thinking that I could represent the story of other people's conflicts. But I knew the power of theatre to create change and to move people to understanding. I wanted to use theatre but I needed to make sure that the people were telling their own stories. The search for this kind of theatre led me straight to Augusto Boal. I found his work intriguing, inspiring, and felt at once a call to do something with it. I received excellent training in the techniques of Theatre of the Oppressed from Marc Weinblatt in Port Townsend, Washington.

I then applied this training to the facilitation skills and techniques I learned and practiced in my doctoral course work and my dissertation research. This marriage of the training and application of those skills with my research in Conflict Analysis and Resolution gave rise to the process described in this book, Dramatic Problem Solving.

Introduction

Dramatic Problem Solving (DPS) is a systematic approach to conflict transformation through a series of simultaneously fun and serious exercises. The process combines group facilitation processes with a series of performance and theatre-based exercises to generate thought, analysis, and action around an issue and/or conflict chosen by the group. The model is a method for creating the space where conflicts and problems that individuals, groups, organizations, and communities are facing can be discussed and transformed in an interactive, fun, emotional, and profound way. The goal is to unearth the roots of the problem, discover and discuss the undiscussable topics surrounding the conflict, and by working together on agreed-upon actions, make change.

This book is designed to provide a straightforward, practical guide on how to use the DPS techniques. It can be used by anyone who works with groups of people and is interested in facilitating conflict transformation and change in those groups. The process draws on various academic and practical disciplines and philosophies. Among them are humanism, feminism, performance studies, anthropology, education, facilitation, and conflict resolution. In this way the work seeks a true praxis, actions that are informed by research that is informed cyclically by direct actions. Through a series of exercises, discussions, performances, and action plans, individuals, groups, and communities can analyze their conflicts and create real, lasting transformative changes. DPS has been used in a wide variety of settings, including schools, universities, non-governmental organizations (NGOs), private companies, prisons, and different communities. It is a conflict resolution tool for group building, organizational change, community development, facilitated problem solving, and personal growth. DPS is a process that has been used in elementary and high schools, universities, communities, NGOs, and prisons. The DPS model has been used in Costa Rica, Nicaragua, Panama, the United States, Kenya, and Ecuador. Also, people from various backgrounds have come together for a week of training on how to facilitate and implement the DPS model. The process has brought together people from distinct languages, cultures, socio-economic backgrounds, spiritual beliefs, and regions of the world to help us all realize that we all have conflicts. We all have many of the same conflicts and it is through moving, watching, and listening to each other can we come together to create transformation in our lives and in our world.

The results of the process have been seen at both a personal and organizational level. Individuals develop new awareness of their beliefs about issues, their abilities to problem solve, and how to be a valuable member of a team that is working to successfully achieve a goal and transform a conflict. At the same time, the community or organizational groups create change through concrete actions. Action planning is a key step in the process and participants in the workshops and community members work together to implement and follow-up on the action plans. Developmentally, the process works to leave behind a core set of skills and leaders for confronting and transforming conflicts in the future. The goal of good facilitation and community development is to not be needed any more. The processes and skills developed in the workshops and classes you facilitate become ingrained in the communities and behaviors of those you work with. The best feeling a facilitator can have is when he or she is no longer needed by a community or group to deal with conflict.

The techniques work by getting people to move out of their chairs and, simultaneously their reliance on verbal expression. Beginning with the use of physical and non-verbal expression and later adding verbal analysis, groups dynamically analyze and contemplate changes to the conflicts they are confronting. The exercises in the DPS model are designed to engage all members of the group in sharing their thoughts, feelings, and alternatives for the topic under consideration. Therefore, it must include all types of learners and expressers. It is a facilitation model in which in every exercise the goal is to have every voice heard, and every person's perspective on the question posed or conflict analyzed, seen and heard. It is the visual and kinesthetic aspect of the work that allows for it to be more democratic than a solely verbal approach to group facilitation. Participants do not have to be actors nor the facilitators dramatic directors, instead the process allows for people to get in touch with their intuitive, visceral, physical response and analysis of a conflict. This allows people to think in new ways, see things from new perspectives, and try out novel behaviors in a safe environment. Creating that space for exploration of the different, the fresh in a space that is liminal, neither totally in the reality of the community nor out of it, but on the threshold, is key for the success of DPS.

The Dramatic Problem Solving process comes out of the Theatre of the Oppressed techniques developed by Augusto Boal. Beginning in the 1950s, and throughout the 1960s and 1970s, a wave of popular education movements hit South America. Led by Paolo Freire and others, the educators came to the people prepared to provide them with education based upon their specific culture and needs. Freire called for an end to the banking system of education, where information was deposited into the minds of the students for later withdrawal. He called for a process where the students became the generators of knowledge, and the teacher the facilitator. This leveling of education, creating a dialogic relationship between the teacher and student was revolutionary in that it sought to empower people by teaching them the skills they identified as necessary not the ones brought to them in a packaged curriculum from the state. At this same time, also in Brazil, a theatre director named Augusto Boal was utilizing the same ideas of the dialogic and the leveling of the relationship between the actor and the spectator, the director and the actor.

Boal, working out of Sao Paolo and later in Argentina and Chile when exiled by the Brazilian government, worked with populations to expose the oppressive situations they were living. He created and used theatre games and exercises, to build performances that grew out of news headlines, images, and dialogues. This took various forms, including invisible theatre, image theatre, and forum theatre. These techniques and performance style form what Boal has called the "arsenal" of the Theatre of the Oppressed (TO).

When Boal published his book *Theatre of the Oppressed* in 1978, he put into writing the work he had been doing in South America over the previous two decades. The central concept was to transform what was from a Greek, Aristotelian theatre that perpetuated the status quo, to a Brechtian theatre that involved the audience and provoked them to think, to, finally, a popular theatre of non-actors taking the stage in practice for revolution, rehearsing change in their lives. For a more complete description of the process of TO, begin by reading *Theatre of the Oppressed* (1978) and then move on to *The Rainbow of Desire* (2000) and *Legislative Theatre* (1998), for a look at the ways Boal has mutated, transformed, and applied TO in many different contexts. Worldwide, people have taken this work and transmuted it and applied it in novel ways to help their own communities confront and transform conflict.

DPS also uses the facilitated group problem solving and change methods described by Roger Schwarz in his book *The Skilled Facilitator* (2002). This structure asks groups to use a nine-step process to identify and clearly define the issue to be discussed. The root causes are examined. Then, the group generates, evaluates, and selects alternative solutions to the conflict. These selected alternatives are placed in a concrete action plan that is implemented and reviewed. Each of the nine steps of the process is gone through with exercises that are suitable to that step's question. The exercises come from various places, experiences, and sources I was aware of. A storytelling exercise from the work of Wil Weigler, a concept definition technique I learned in my graduate studies in education, several games from my time as an improvisational comedy troupe member, and other new inventions and adaptations from my experiences were all added to the set of exercises developed and practiced by Boal and practitioners doing TO work throughout the world.

DPS also utilizes the cyclical structure of action research and experiential education. The format of look, think, act, review, re-look, re-think, re-act is utilized in the full model. Below is a graphic representation of the DPS model in terms of the action research model.

DPS participatory action research process

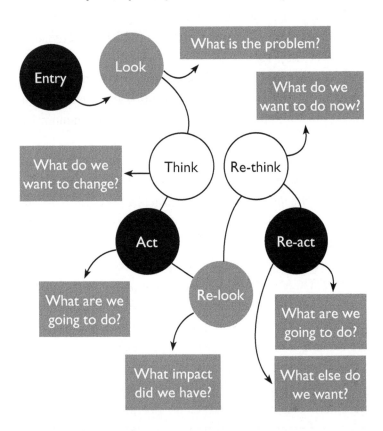

In the DPS process the evocative emotional outlet that theatre-based exercises provide is combined with a logical and structured approach to conflict transformation that is designed to build success and leave behind groups with new skills for confronting their conflicts.

The book can be used to guide a start to finish approach to working with one group or as a reference for activities that can be applied in different contexts. This manual presents a step-by-step breakdown of the way TO and the other exercises are utilized within the Schwarz problem solving model. The concepts of humanism, action research, and experiential education are interwoven throughout the descriptions and explanations of the process. The process is a framework, a guide for facilitated problem solving with groups. It is presented in a step-by-step format. However, the process and steps and the exercises to use are not set in stone. Some of these exercises can be used alone to work on a specific issue. The warm-ups and closings are good with any group. Image theatre alone or forum theatre alone can be a great tool. Other exercises or steps that would be more appropriate based upon the age of the group members, the physical capabilities of the group, the culture of the group, or your personal experience and skills as a facilitator can be added or substituted. The hope is to present a series of techniques that will result in a positive change in the lives of those who participate in the process.

CHAPTER I

Beginnings

Starting work with a group is one of the most important points in facilitation. Many times a facilitator will be coming from the outside to work with the group. We may know no one or only one person in the room. People may not be aware of what the process will be and apprehensions can abound in the group. This is especially true with this process because people often feel intimidated when you use words like "theatre" and "acting." Feelings of anxiety about everyone looking at them and having to remember lines can be strong and lead to blocking on the part of participants. Therefore, developing rapport, a sense of ease and acceptance within the group, is essential. In the Dramatic Problem Solving process we ask people to share honestly and look deeply. Group cohesion is something that will grow as the process unfolds but these beginning stages are where the tone is set.

We begin with exercises designed to accomplish several things. First is to get to know the names of the participants. Second, to get people used to the idea that during the process they are going to be moving their bodies to express themselves physically. Third, to see what some unseen commonalities and differences are in the group. We begin to do some physical work as a group. Finally, we begin to look at how we think about conflicts and ways to transform them in our lives.

A key point to stress is that while we are here to work on serious issues, it is important to also have fun.

Welcome exercises

 WELCOME CIRCLE

- Begin by having everyone stand or sit in a circle.

- Welcome everyone and thank everyone for coming and being willing to participate in this important process.

- Say that we are going to begin by being together with each other in silence. The silence serves to center the group, bring the spirit of the group together into the space, calm everyone and bring them into the present.

- The silence lasts from three to five minutes.

- When the silence is broken ask for brief comments about how the silence felt.

- Stress the importance of the ability to be silent: to hear others, to hear yourself, to hear the group.

- This exercise is a great way to begin any meeting or group exercise. Silence is something that is often missing in the buzz of our daily lives. Bringing everyone together in a circle of silence helps to create that liminal, ritual space that a workshop can provide. This is a space where new things can happen.

- Silence makes the energy of the group more palpable and everyone becomes aware of each other. This is what happens in those moments between lines in a theatre play. That energy is there and the ritual space is created. We hope we can use the energy in positive ways.

 ## NAME PLAYBACK CIRCLE

This exercise utilizes the "playback" technique used so effectively in Playback Theatre (for more on Playback, see Jonathan Fox's *Acts of Service*). This is a fun exercise and a great way to break the ice, learn names, and also help people identify what they hope to get out of being a part of this process.

- Participants all stand in a circle.
- Each person takes their turn, going around the circle.
- Each person steps forward one step into the circle, states their name, makes a gesture with their body (encourage that bigger is always better) and states one word or phrase that goes along with that gesture. The word or phrase should describe what they hope to get from this Dramatic Problem Solving experience or the meeting or the class or whatever is appropriate for your setting. The question could be, "What do you

hope to learn during our time together?" or "What is your main reason for being here?"

- When the person has stated their name, made the gesture and word or phrase, that person steps back into their spot in the circle.

- Then, everyone else in the group takes one step forward into the circle, looks directly at the person who just stated their name, gesture, and word/phrase, and does exactly what they just did. Then, they repeat the same thing.

- Each person takes a turn stating their name, gesture, and word/phrase and having it played back for them.

- When everyone has gone you can ask for a brief comment or two about how people felt in that exercise.

- This exercise helps people relax. It is also a beginning exploration of how one can express feelings, hopes, and motivations in a physical way; combining the verbalization and the physicalization. It is also a way for people to see themselves; observing the way others interpret their words, body language, and expressions.

Adaptations: If it is a group you are familiar with or continuing to work with, you can change the question that drives the gesture-word. Some examples are, "What is something we don't know about you?" or you can ask them to think of any positive quality they have.

Also, you can simply have the participants make a sound to go with their gesture. This is especially helpful with children.

❀ COVER THE SPACE

This exercise is one of the quintessential Boal group movement, group cohesion, physical space awareness warm-ups that is part of any Theatre of the Oppressed work done anywhere. After a time with a group, the facilitator will not direct the participants to "walk around the room" or "move about freely" but instead to "cover the space."

The basic concept is that everyone is working to continually move around the space you are working in while maintaining the space equally covered at all times.

- Ask everyone to begin walking around and exploring the space they will be working in.

- Call out for the participants to "cover the space." Clear limits of what the space you are working in should be set. The size of the group and space will determine how much or how little of the space you will use. But, traditionally you try to cover the whole space.

- Participants move at a normal pace around the space, working to maintain it, so that it is covered equally at all times.

- After 30 seconds of moving, Clap your hands and call out, "Freeze." Everyone freezes and examines how they are in terms of having the space covered evenly.

- Participants begin moving again. Then randomly call out "Freeze."

- Have the group move at a faster or slower speed.

- It is important to emphasize, through comments during the exercise, the function of this exercise as a way of making the group more cohesive. Use prompts such as, "Where do you need to be to help the group right now," and "Standing still only makes others have to work harder," and "Work as individuals to make the group cover the space."

- This is a silent exercise; participants should not be talking. They should be encouraged to focus on what their role in the group is.

- After a few minutes of starting and stopping, ask the group for comments about the exercise. Keep it brief.

Variation: When the participants freeze, they have five seconds to move slowly and silently to cover the space evenly.

 SOCIOMETRY

Sociometry is a way of visually and physically representing the make up or feelings of a group. The technique comes out of psychodrama and the work of Jakob Moreno. This is a great exercise that can be used to answer almost any question. It gets people up and moving. It provides an avenue of expression for the less verbal people in the group, perhaps revealing a silent majority. It can be used as a check-in tool with the group to ask where people are with the process in terms of clarity, direction, and process. As a beginning exercise it is used to break the ice and show unseen commonalities and differences in the group. We then begin a dialogue around conflict.

- Begin by explaining that we are going to take a physical survey using something called sociometry.

- Ask the participants to place themselves physically on a map of the world showing where each of them was born. This is often very interesting when various countries and regions are overrepresented to note how much space that country or region takes up in the world.

- Each person then tells where they were born.

- Ask them to move to where they live now. Some people move and others do not. (In one workshop done with Nicaraguan immigrants in Costa Rica, it was a really important and profound moment when the whole group left Nicaragua together to come to Costa Rica.)

- Again, each person tells where they currently live.

- Next, draw an imaginary line down the middle of the room. This is a continuum. The continuum represents spectrum of how the people in the group feel about conflict.

- At one end of the spectrum are people who avoid conflict at all costs.

- At the other end of the spectrum are people who thrive on conflict and even seek it.

- People can place themselves along the continuum wherever they see themselves dealing with conflict in their lives.

- Ask people to be honest with themselves and think about how they really are and not how they wish they were.

- People can then speak about why they are where they are along the continuum.

- This demonstrates that there are various approaches to conflicts and that not everyone has the same feeling about them.

- The importance for the work done in the DPS workshop is that we all must be ready to look at the conflicts in our lives honestly and collaboratively.

This leads to the next activity, which is Agreement Making.

 ## AGREEMENT MAKING

It is essential for any group to have a set of agreements; guidelines and ground rules for the group members' behaviors and ways of being that everyone agrees are necessary for the group to work well. Some facilitators begin with a set of ground rules or agreements and ask participants to add any they think are important. In the DPS process, it is important that ownership of the whole process is given to the participants. Also, consensus building can begin now. The group begins to learn to work together to make decisions. It is a good time as a facilitator to see the group dynamics; leaders surface, fighters emerge, those who speak most eloquently are identified, and you will notice the people who are quieter.

When making agreements it is important to phrase them in concrete, positive language. Avoid "Don't…" and "No…" Instead phrase things in terms of the positive behaviors the group wants to see exhibited throughout the process. I always include three things that may or may not come up. These are: (1) have fun; (2) push yourself beyond your comfort zone; and (3) everyone has the right to pass.

Write all of the agreements, trying to limit them to five to eight agreements, on a large piece of paper and display them in a place in the room where they will be for all of the sessions. The participants and the facilitator can return to the agreements to call people on behavior, other agreements can be added, or existing ones modified as the process unfolds.

CHAPTER 2

Defining the Problem

Once the ice has been broken and the agreements have been reached it is time to begin to define the problem or problems the group would like to focus on. A series of exercises are done to find out what possible conflicts are to be addressed and then to narrow them down to one or two that have the most attraction for the whole group.

 COLOMBIAN HYPNOSIS

We begin with this classic Boal technique for a number of reasons. It is a great theatre exercise in itself, teaching to let go, accept, and give and take. It is also a great metaphor for communication, especially in the third step of the exercise. It is at the same time a physical demonstration of the way we are controlled in our lives by forces that are so big they seem insurmountable, to the point of seeming invisible forces beyond our control. The direction to the followers to consider ways to follow without wanting to, to resist, comes from Marc Weinblatt and it is a great addition.

Here is where the process of conscientization begins. A discussion of this concept (see Freire, 1973) is important in the debriefing of this exercise.

- Have the group divide into partners.

- The partners decide who is A and who is B.

- The partner A will begin as the hypnotist and B the hypnotized.

- Ask for a volunteer to work with you to demonstrate the process, which is as follows.

- The hypnotist holds his or her hand about eight inches away from the face of the hypnotized. The hand is the instrument of control.

- The hypnotized must follow the hand wherever it goes, always maintaining it the same eight-inch distance from his or her face.

- The hypnotist can move around the room, moving his or her body up, down, around, and wherever he or she feels comfortable.

- After the demonstration, the partners begin the exercise.

- Give the instruction to focus on the hand; it is all important.

- After a minute or two of hypnosis, instruct the followers to try to think of ways they can follow without really following, to resist the hand.

- Then switch the direction to the idea that following the hand is life and death.

- The hypnotist then brings their partner out of the trance.

- Switch partners, giving the same instructions.

- Once both partners have been hypnotized the next step is that both partners are the hypnotized and the hypnotizer, simultaneously.

- They must maintain their face eight inches from the hand of their partner while also giving messages with their hand to their partner.

- Instruct the partners to find a way to end their mutual trance.

- Follow with a discussion featuring the following questions, and others as you see fit:

  In one word or two, how did it feel to be led?

  In one word or two, how did it feel to be the leader?

  Who found it easier to lead? To follow?

  Where in your life do you see any times when you are following?

  What are the hands in your life?

- Following this discussion, which will doubtless open up some ideas about what conflicts people would like to confront but aren't, the group is ready to look at naming some problems.

❋ BRAINSTORM – WHAT'S THE PROBLEM?

This brainstorming session is a wide-open exploration of what issues, conflicts, and problems people in the group want to work on.

- Begin by setting ground rules for brainstorming, these include:

    reserving judgment

    anything goes

    save the deeper discussion for later.

- Write down everyone's ideas on a large piece of paper in the front of the room.

- Review the list orally and ask if there are any issues that aren't on the list that need to be there.

- Once the brainstorm list is generated, ask the group to begin to think about which of those has the most "heat" or "energy" for them. Which one do they feel most passionate about working on and seeing changed?

❋ DUELING IMAGES

Based on the brainstormed list, the group can begin to explore which issues, conflicts, or problems they want to confront. This is where the first exercises that come out of Boal's image theatre are utilized. This variation, Dueling Images, comes from Marc Weinblatt. It is a good, fun way to open image work.

- Begin with the whole group together as one. Tell the group you are going to begin work with images to express and define problems.

- State to the group some basic emotion words that everyone can relate to and ask them to form a statue or image that, for them, represents that word. Words like "love" "peace" and "anger" or "hate" tend to work well. You can also throw out the name of a current political figure or political issue to get them thinking of how to represent something outside of themselves.

- Divide the group into groups of six to eight. If the group is only six or eight people, divide the group in half.

- Now each group works together, in silence, to define whatever issue, conflict, or problem the facilitator states.

- Read one of the items from the brainstorm list and tell the group to, in silence, and in 10 to 15 seconds, form a frozen image that represents that issue.

- When all of the groups have formed their image, go one by one unfreezing the groups so they can observe the images created by the other groups.

- Next, choose another item from the brainstorm list and have the groups create another image. This time, once they are frozen, ask them to think about who their character or representation is.

- Go around to each group in turn and ask each person in the statue to tell the group who or what they are.

- Next, state another item and once the image is formed and the character or representation set, ask the people to think about what is the interior monologue of their character in that image. What is that character thinking?

- Everyone speaks their interior monologue at the same time.

- Go around to each person in the groups and have them share their interior monologue.

- Next, do all of the above with another one of the items from the list and ask one character from each image the question, "What is your secret thought? Something you would never share with anyone, ever."

- Ask the group if there are any items on the list that haven't been looked at yet that they feel should be imaged.

- Complete the duelling image process for any items that the group wants.

Now the group has listed some of the issues and physicalized and verbalized some of their components. It is time to narrow down which problem the group is going to focus on.

 SNOWBALL FIGHT

In order to evaluate the options for problems to work on, there needs to be a group decision-making process. This exercise, taken from an icebreaker I learned a long time ago in Hawaii, is a fun way to take a vote as a first step towards narrowing the group's focus.

- Each person takes three sheets of paper (preferably old, reusable paper with print on one side).

- Each person writes one of the items that they feel is the most important to work on in the group over the next few sessions. They write one on each paper, three in total.

- Each person crumples their three papers up into balls, ready for a snowball fight.

- Everyone throws their snowballs at each other and all around the room.

- After a few minutes of this great fun (everyone will be running and laughing), stop the group and have everyone gather up three snowballs, not necessarily the ones that they wrote. In fact it is better for the process if everyone has everyone else's papers.

- One by one, the papers are opened and read. Place a tally mark next to the issue or conflict on the brainstorm list.

- When all of the papers have been read, count the number of tally marks to make sure that everyone's paper has been shared.

- Review the results of the tallying. The ones with the most tally marks should be the issue or issue the group will then begin to work on in-depth.

Clarify with the group, making sure that this issue is the one and not one that suddenly occurs to them or one that received a few less votes. Perhaps the real issue is a grouping of two or three issues that received one or two votes each, but if we put them together, it is where the real energy of the group lies. This is still a consensus process, just using voting as a way of eliminating some ideas and providing more clarity as to which issues are of highest importance.

It is important to note that while not all issues a group has are going to be looked at during this particular process, it does not mean that those issues are not worth looking at. Perhaps another session can be scheduled for working specifically on the second or third highest vote getter. Or a smaller section of the group may want to focus on that problem in a separate session. It may also be that after some time working on the issue chosen, the group realizes that the real problem is X, Y, or Z, and that is what will be the focus. The important thing is to be flexible and also give respect and space to everyone's ideas.

CHAPTER 3

Analyzing the Issue

Now the issue is named and accepted as the focus point for the group. The next step is to explore what is really at the heart of the problem. So, the next activities are designed to examine how the problem is seen in the daily lives of the people through stories and images. Following that, the group will explore the root causes of the conflict, looking below the surface. Finally a written definition will emerge to provide even greater clarity as to what the issue is, who is involved in it, and what the root causes of it are.

 STORYTELLING

This particular storytelling exercise comes from Wil Weigler's book *Strategies for Playbuilding* (2001). It is a very good way of getting people to listen to each other, think about the way the problem appears in their lives, and to begin to think of dramatic presentations of the problem. I have added a Boalian component with the image making as the final step in the "unpacking" of the story, to use Weigler's term.

- All of the papers from the snowball fight that have the top one or two vote getters or the issues chosen by the group are placed in a pile in the center of the circle the group has formed.

- Each person, in turns, chooses one of the papers and reads the issue written on it.

- The person then has 30 seconds to a minute to think of something from their life, a story they can tell about this issue, a way it has affected them.

- Before the person begins the story, instruct the group to be listening very actively because when the person finishes the group is going to unpack and analyze the story.

- The person tells their story and everyone listens.

- When the person has finished, analyze the story by asking the following questions:

  1. What words or phrases stood out in the story, what was said?

  2. What movements or gestures stood out, what actions did you see?

  3. What sounds did you hear in the story?

  4. What is this story like, what is a simile for this story?

  5. What is the opposite of the story?

  6. What is the comedy version of the story?

  7. What is the musical version of the story?

  8. What is the image of the story? Here ask the

storyteller to sculpt an image of the story they told. You can also have them or someone else sculpt the opposite.

- This continues until everyone who would like to tell a story has done so.

This is a time-consuming process, and requires more time sitting and listening than any other part of the process. However, it is an invaluable tool to refer back through as the process gets into later stages. The facilitator can refer back to the notes of what words, sounds, images, and actions stood out in the stories to help inform the scenes that will be created. Therefore, it is essential to take notes on the story unpacking for later reference.

Before going on to the next phase, which is analysis of the root causes, it is important to do some group building and trust work to establish group cohesion and also eliminate some apprehensions about self-expression in the group.

 MEMORY GAME

This is an exercise that I invented while sitting at the dinner table with a group of workshop participants. My son Sam asked if we could play memory. I said sure and invented this game on the spot. It has turned into a favorite of groups because it focuses on something positive, and the way the individual and the group are connected.

- Have everyone sit in a circle.

- Ask everyone to close their eyes and to think of a time when they were very happy.

- They should focus on a specific memory, a time and a place.

- Ask them to be in that memory and to notice where they are, who is with them, if anyone, and what the colors, sounds, and other objects are around them. These are the parts of their memory.

- Then, ask everyone to open their eyes and be back in the group space.

- Then, going around the circle one at a time each person will share one element from their memory, just one element not the whole thing.

- When someone shares an element, ask anyone else who had that as part of their memory to raise their hand. Examples include trees, music, the ocean, etc.

- Continue around the circle adding more elements until you have gone around the circle two or three times. At this point everyone should have several elements revealed because of what they had in common with the other memories.

- The group will then try to guess each person's memory.

- Each person tells the story of their memory and why it was a happy or important time for them.

- When all the memories have been shared, conclude with an applause and have everyone stand up and stretch.

This exercise is one that I have used to point out the fact that while we all have distinct pasts and memories, and that we are all individuals; we have a great deal in common. The important learning for the group is to see that through the process they are going through they are going to come with their individual pasts, find some things in common, and create something new. We are all parts of a whole that is made up of old and new ideas.

 SWEDISH MULTIPLE SCULPTURE

This is a technique from Boal. I don't know why it is called Swedish, probably because Boal invented or adapted the game while working in Sweden or with someone Swedish. Anyway, the exercise works like this.

- Everyone chooses a partner.
- Decide who is partner A and partner B.
- This is a "blind" exercise, meaning that people will be working with their eyes closed. It is important to remind everyone to cross their arms in front of them to provide safety bumpers while moving around with their eyes closed.
- Partner A will begin sighted and Partner B will be blind.
- Partner B follows the call of his or her name as Partner A calls his or her name and moves around the room.
- The sighted partners should try calling their partner's name from various distances, at various volumes, and play with their tone and sound of voice.

- Then, after a minute or two of following the name, the facilitator calls freeze.

- All of the sighted partners move to where their partners are and take them, still blind, to a central point in the room.

- Once all of the blind people are together, the sighted partners work, always in silence, to create a group sculpture. Each sighted partner sculpts his or her blind partner as a part of a large image. Encourage the sculptors to be as specific as possible with their placement of hands, feet, legs, and whole body.

- Next, the sighted partners must stand together in front of their sculptures and, again in silence; create the mirror image of their sculptures using their own bodies. Each sighted person takes the form of their blind partner.

- When the sighted partners have finished their mirror image, the blind sculpture, maintaining their eyes closed, comes apart and each blind person must search and find their partner in the mirror image of the sculpture they were just a part of.

- Once everyone has found their partner, and verified by asking them their name, everyone opens their eyes and sees the mirror image of the sculpture.

- Repeat the process with partner A now blind and Partner B sighted.

- Follow-up with a discussion about the importance of trust and the need to rely on other senses. Our culture is so visual and so dependent on seeing exactly what is happening that it is very important to stop and take time to use other senses to discover things. In this way we can begin to open other pathways and seek new ways of thinking about our lives and our problems.

CHAPTER 4

What do We Want to See?

In order to get to a place of conflict transformation, we have to establish what it is that we envision as that change. In the following process, we ask the group to define what the solution should include and should work to achieve. To complete this and help establish criteria for a resolution, we use an exercise called 1-3-2 Thinking.

 1-3-2 THINKING

- Ask one volunteer to step out into the circle and offer an image of the conflict, or at least one aspect of the conflict, that he or she would like to focus on.

- The volunteer creates a sculpted image using the other members of the group to show what the problem is.

- The volunteer explains the image to the group.

- The volunteer then takes the same people and sculpts them in an image of the ideal, or how they wish the conflict would look.

- The volunteer then explains the ideal image to the group.

- The volunteer then sculpts the people in the ideal image in a new image that shows one or a series of actions that need to happen in order to transform the first image into the third image.

- The volunteer explains the image.

- Ask the group to think about what other actions could be taken and if there are volunteers to create a new action.

- A new volunteer who focuses on a different aspect of the conflict or a different ideal image can repeat this process.

This exercise helps the group be able to think about solutions. There are no judgments or action planning attached to the steps shown to get from 1 to 3. However, this exercise shows the importance of not only knowing what the problem is but what you would like the solution to look like.

This exercise of 1-3-2 Thinking can also be used as a stand-alone exercise to work with a group in a short session designed to stimulate dialogue and actions.

CHAPTER 5

What are the Root Causes of the Problem?

Now that the trust level of the group is deeper, we can begin to go a bit deeper into the problems the group is ready to transform. We will begin to explore the root causes.

 TWO SECRETS OF ST TERESA

This is an improvisational theatre game designed to help actors work on developing tension, explore relationship and resolve multiple problems. I use it here because I have found it a way of beginning the exploration of what is at the root of the issue. The game involves two people in a permanent relationship, (e.g. mother–son, brother–sister), and each of them has a secret they have kept from each other. During the exercise each of them reveals their secret and the pair have to deal with both secrets. This exercise is useful at this point for many reasons. It is the first exercise that involves "acting" and the acting is all done in pairs while no one is watching. This provides a safe space for people to try out some acting without feeling totally self-conscious. This is important because it is placed at the "root causes" portion of the process, and it deals with secrets. When we analyze community, family, and personal conflicts we often find that it is the things that people are not supposed to discuss, things that remain hidden from view and discussion that are at the root of the problem. So, we begin by having people think of a secret related to the problem we are dealing with, something someone would hide from another person related to the issue.

- Divide the group into pairs.

- Have the partners determine a relationship, like father–son, mother–daughter, or siblings, something that they cannot get out of. This is important to the exercise because it forces them to make choices to deal with the problem. If the relationship is an impermanent one, such as friends, or even spouses, there is always the option to say, "Well, I am leaving now and I will never see you again." This is not really a choice in close family relationships; sure it happens, but it is much less common than divorce or the end of a friendship.

- Once the relationship is established, have each party think of a secret they might be keeping from their partner. The secret should have something to do with the problem as defined by the group.

- Next have the partners decide on the definition of the central questions of theatre scene making: Where are you? When is it? Why are you there?

- Tell them that at a certain point you are going to call out, "First Secret." At that point one of the partners will divulge their secret. The other partner must then deal with the secret.

- The other person who did not share their secret must wait until the facilitator calls "Second Secret." The other now tells their secret. Both secrets are now in play and must be dealt with.

- The scenes begin and the two secrets are called for.

- Instruct the partners after a few minutes to find a point of resolution to their scenes.

- When all the scenes are finished, have all of the partners share with the larger group what their relationship, secrets, and resolution was.

- Watch for commonalities among secrets. These things that people choose to hide or feel that should be kept secret about the issue are often the "elephant in the room" that everyone sees but no one wants to talk about, because to go there would require some serious work and problem solving.

- Based upon this first exploration of the secrets kept about the problem, the group can begin to think about what other things are root causes of the problem.

Root cause brainstorm and sculptures

Ask the group to think about all of the things they see as root causes of the conflict or problem you are exploring.

Write down all of the suggestions, following the rules of brainstorming: reserving judgment, refrain from analyzing deeply, speaking for yourself, anything goes.

Post the paper with all of the root causes in a prominent place in the room.

Review the list of brainstormed root causes orally with the group. Now we will use more detailed sculpting exercises. Sculpting is a way for someone to use the bodies of others to physically express their ideas and opinions on a subject.

 ## SCULPTING

- Ask for volunteers to create a human sculpture of one of the root causes. Ask the question, "What does this look like?" "Who and what is involved?"

- One person comes forth and, using as few or as many people as he or she needed, creates a sculpture of one of the root causes.

- When sculpting there are basic rules: it is done in silence as much as possible.

- The people being sculpted must be relaxed and try to actually be "like clay" for the sculptors.

- The sculptors need to give clear messages, make strong choices.

- Don't forget the face. What does this person's face look like? This is an important part of sculpting that people often forget.

- Sculptors can demonstrate how they want the person to look by using their own body or by moving them with their hands. A combination is also effective.

- When the sculpture is done, have it stay still for a few moments in silence before asking the sculptor to explain it.

- When the sculptor has finished explaining their sculpture, ask for feedback from the group.

- Anyone who wishes to create a root cause sculpture can do so. The same root cause can be repeated but it is helpful to look at several. This helps the group really begin to narrow their focus. Now they have the issue as well as the exact root causes for which they wish to focus on designing transformative changes.

Building greater trust: Blind exercises

As the process goes deeper into the exploration of the conflict, it is going to require a great deal of trust within the group for all of the issues to be discussed, for everyone to feel accepted and comfortable. To that end it is important to insert various trust building and group cohesion exercises in the process. Here is a good time to do some work with other "Blind" exercises: Blind Hugs and Handshakes, and Cars.

 BLIND HUGS AND HANDSHAKES

In this exercise, partners try to reconnect while not being able to see each other.

- Have everyone find a partner, preferably someone they have not worked with yet or that they do not normally work with.

- The partners stand close and face each other.

- Everyone closes their eyes.

- The partners all shake hands while keeping their eyes closed.

- As you count from one to seven, the partners take one step backwards away from each other for each number counted.

- When you reach seven everyone stops.

- Count backward from seven to one.

- The partners take one step towards each other for each number counted off.

- The partners try to return to a handshaking position when you reach the one.

- Repeat the same exercise only this time the partners begin by hugging each other and then try to find the hug.

 BLIND CARS

This exercise, which is really good for letting go and trusting as well as practising giving and receiving messages, is a fun and lively way to help people let go of some of their inhibitions about being led. It really helps build group cohesion.

- Have everyone find a partner; different from the one they just completed blind hugs with.
- The partners decide who will begin as the *car* and who the *driver*.
- The cars will be "blind cars" maintaining their eyes closed while being driven by their drivers.
- The drivers will drive their cars from behind with five simple signals to give their cars to make them go.
- If the driver presses with their index finger between the shoulder blades of the car, the car moves forward. The harder the pressure, the faster the car goes.
- If the driver presses on the left shoulder, the car turns to the left.
- If the driver presses on the right shoulder, the car turns to the right.
- If the driver presses on the lower back of the car, the car backs up.
- If the driver removes their finger from the car, the car stops.
- Cars cross their elbows in front of them to make bumpers.
- Everyone begins driving their cars at once.
- After a few minutes, ask the drivers to park their cars.
- The drivers and cars switch roles.
- Repeat the exercise with the new cars and drivers.

Follow this exercise up with a brief discussion of the importance of letting go and accepting the messages you get as we move into creating a dramatic presentation of the problem. Also, talk about whether or not it was easier to be driven or to drive. This often allows you to see who the leaders in the group are. People often report not liking driving because they don't like the responsibility. Others don't like the car role because they have a hard time giving up that much control to another person. There are a number of ways to deal with this exercise. It is used here mainly for a fun way to build trust in the group. If you were doing this exercise in group therapy you could explore all kinds of issues around trust, authority, and anything else that might comes up. However, if this is group problem solving, then it is important to maintain focus on the problem, issue, and conflict at hand for the entire group.

CHAPTER 6

Creating Clarity and Consensus

This phase in the process focuses on clearly defining what it is that the group wants to present as the core problem. This will help to create a clear consensus among the group as to what exactly it is that the group wants to see changed in their world. Clarity of expression and narrowing of thought is fundamental to this portion. We do exercises focused on being clear, getting what you want and thinking about the attributes and non-attributes of the issue. Now that the root causes have been identified we can move past some of the talking around the problem and get into the generation of knowledge about the problem that is novel and to the point. This is an important discussion because as Schwarz points out in his rules for effective groups, it is important to "discuss undiscussables." We did a forum play one time where there was a cardboard elephant that kept getting passed around; whoever had the problem had the elephant, but no one talked about it or recognized it. This is the elephant in the room people often talk about. We must not only look at the elephants or problems in our lives but also deal with them in new, creative ways.

 PERUVIAN BALL GAME

This is a very old theatre exercise that stresses the importance of making clear choices and effective non-verbal communication. The importance of being specific, clarifying to make sure your message is understood and that you also understood the information you were given are integral parts of the process.

- Everyone begins to Cover the Space.

- As the participants move about the space, each of them begins to play with an imaginary ball.

- The shape, size, texture, and function of the ball should be very clear in their actions.

- After a minute or two defining their ball and its properties each person must find someone to trade balls with.

- When they trade it is important to make sure they demonstrate exactly how to play with the ball and have it demonstrated back to them by the recipient and vice versa.

- They then begin to Cover the Space playing with their new ball.

- After about 30 seconds with the new ball, everyone finds another person and exchanges balls again.

- After playing with the second ball a short while, they find another partner and trade balls once more.

- Now, everyone begins to Cover the Space and look for the person that has their original ball.

- When someone has found their original ball, they can take it back, but continue to play with the last ball they had until the original owner comes to collect it.

- When everyone or almost everyone has found their original ball you can begin the verification process.

- Trace back the trading route of the ball they thought was their original. It is interesting to see how balls change and become very different.

- The important thing to stress in this exercise is that if we wish to be understood, especially if we have a novel idea or even an idea that is similar to others but maybe slightly different and unique, it is necessary to take the time to first examine exactly what it is you wish to express. Then make sure there is clear understanding of your idea and how it works, in this case a ball.

 BUYER–SELLER

Now that the group has seen the importance of being clear and how it can work, they will play a game called Buyer–Seller. This improvisational comedy game is used here because it looks at the problem of not being able to speak clearly and directly to the point and how that often results in unfair or unwanted agreements being made.

- Begin by asking for two volunteers.

- Explain how the game works.

- One person is the buyer and the other is the seller.

- The buyer and the seller are buying and selling completely different things, but they don't know it.

- They must complete a transaction.

- They cannot say or be very clear about what it is that they are trying to buy or sell.

- They must accept, using the improv rule of "Yes, and…" that is to say, take what someone gives you, accept it, and then add your own twist to it. Do not block.

- First, the buyer leaves the room or space while the seller remains with the group.

- The group tells the buyer what he or she is shopping for.

- The buyer leaves and sends in the seller.

- The group tells the seller what he or she is selling.

- The scene then begins with the buyer entering the store of the seller.

- They act out the scene and in the end, without expressing what it is that they exactly want to buy or sell, complete a sale.

- It is important to note that this is not a guessing game, the players are not trying to guess what the other is buying or selling. Instead, the focus is on accepting, pleasing, and completing the transaction.

- Invite others to be buyers and sellers.

- When everyone that wants to try the exercise has had a chance to go, or after one or two rounds, depending on your time constraints, have a discussion around the experience of being in that game.

- Key questions to ask are:

    1. What was it like to not be able to say exactly what you wanted to?

    2. How is this similar to situations in life?

    3. Are there things that need to be said that cannot be talked about but everyone accepts them?

    4. Have you ever wound up just accepting an agreement just to make someone happy or just to get it over with and move on?

 FOUR SQUARE DEFINITION OF THE PROBLEM

We will now move into creating a clear, concise working definition of the problem. Looking at the attributes and non-attributes of the issue does this. This is an educational technique that can be used with any topic or concept. The importance of stating what something is not, as well as what it is, helps a great deal as people begin to think about what it is that they actually desire, what is the ideal or alternative solution to the problem. What would it look like if it were different?

- Post a large sheet of paper divided into four quadrants.

- In the upper left quadrant write the name of the problem or issue to be defined.

- In the upper right quadrant draw a + sign. Here you will write down all of the attributes of the problem. What makes up the problem? What does it consist of? What does it look like?

- In the lower left quadrant draw a − sign. Here you will write all of the non-attributes of the problem. What is it not? What does it not consist of? What does it not look like? This can be obvious, like it is not a table or a shoe, but try to get to the point of looking at what is lacking for the problem to be transformed into what we would wish to see.

- In the lower right quadrant write the problem is… Here you will create a working definition of the problem. Try to boil it down to one sentence, maximum two, which incorporates the attributes and non-attributes into a clear description of the problem.

- Review the definition with the group. Ask for clarifying questions and feedback.

Now that the group has a working definition to refer back to, and there is consensus as to which attributes of the problem need to be addressed, the process of creating dramatic, activating scenes can begin.

CHAPTER 7

Who is Involved in the Problem?

Now we can begin to work on creating scenes that depict the issue as it is. This will lead to an exploration of what interventions can be taken to transform the issue. We begin this process by looking first at who are the people who must be part of the scenes if we are to get to the heart of the matter and truly transform the conflict. We begin with a discussion of the theatre and literary concepts of protagonists and antagonists. The protagonist is the person in the play or story who is confronted with problems. He or she is the hero or heroine of the story. The antagonist is the person in the play or story who is the cause or continuant of the problems confronted by the protagonist.

In the early work of Augusto Boal in South America, the protagonists and the antagonists were very clear. There was the poor, landless peasant as the protagonist and the rich politician, landholder, or the army as the antagonist. However, most groups you find nowadays in a globalized world, in urban or even rural settings, are not so clear-cut cases of here are the protagonists and here are the antagonists. There are much more likely to be gray areas where the system of oppression has become so great and embedded that the oppressors have their own oppressors.

Another important concept that comes into play here is the idea of internalized oppression and what Boal has called "The Cop in the Head." Later in the process there will be an examination of what the cops are saying in the heads of the protagonists to keep them caught in the problem. However, now is a good time to introduce the idea that everyone has his or her own oppressors and antagonists and that we can choose to go as deeply as we want into any of these.

Identifying and creating characters

Ask the group to think of all of the people who are involved in the issue. Follow the brainstorm guidelines of anything goes without judgment and not to delve too deeply into the subject at the moment.

After the list is compiled, try to determine which of those people could be used as characters in a representation of the problem. Which ones would be possible protagonists and possible antagonists? Sometimes the participants will identify the character of "me" or "us" as the protagonist or the antagonist in the story. This is an important learning moment and a real opportunity to help people move to understand their own actions and how they are perpetuating or working to transform conflicts in their lives. Then we will bring those characters to life with the exercise, Walk, Stop, Justify.

 WALK, STOP, JUSTIFY

This exercise is designed to get people in touch with the different people who are populating the problem they are working on. One of the main goals of this exercise is to get people to recognize the complex nature of all the parties involved in any conflict. An examination of their interests, their needs, and their histories is necessary in order to move beyond stereotypes and into a more realistic presentation and understanding of all people involved in the problem. Only through realistic portrayals of complex individuals can we truly move towards transformation.

- Participants Cover the Space.

- As they move about the space, ask them to begin to move as one of the people from the brainstormed list of characters.

- They should move in a different way than they normally do, unless they are that person.

- As they move in character ask them to think about what they are doing, why, where, and what is their goal.

- As people begin to move around the space with their character beginning to take shape, ask them some personal questions about the character.

    What is your age?

    What is your gender?

    Are you married?

    Do you have children?

    What are you doing right now?

What would you rather be doing right now?

What are your dreams for the future?

- After the last question, always encouraging the participants to move beyond the stereotypes, call "Freeze."

- Call for everyone to speak their interior monologue, the thoughts of their character out loud, all at once.

- Call "Freeze" after ten seconds of speaking the interior monologue.

- Move around the space and ask some of the group members to share their interior monologues.

- Ask them for their age, gender, occupation, hopes.

- Ask some of the characters for their secret thought. Do not do this with everyone, but it is important that everyone has developed some secrets for their character. Return again to the idea of what is hidden as often being at the root of the problem.

- After talking to a few of the characters, have the participants let go of that character. Call, "Shake off that character, you are no longer a _____, you are now a _____," and call for another character from the brainstorm list.

- Repeat the same steps from above with the new character.

- Do this for five or six of the characters that seem to be the most important to the problem. Use both protagonist types and antagonists so that everyone in the group can have a chance to walk a few footsteps in the shoes of the both the protagonist and the antagonist.

 MULTIPLE IMAGES OF OPPRESSION

Now the group is ready to examine some ways that this problem is played out by the characters. The conflict resolution concepts of needs, interests, and positions will now be explored through an exercise in which people are working to get what they want, to meet their interests while being confronted by the needs and interests of others.

- Begin by reviewing the name of the problem, its definition, some of the sights and sounds from the stories, the root causes, and the characters from the brainstorm list. This review helps center the group.

- Ask for three volunteers to be image sculptors.

- Ask the volunteers which aspect of the problem they would like to focus on.

- Divide into three groups based upon interest in the aspect each sculptor will be working on.

- If you have a small group of six, you can have two groups of three or if the group is large, you can have four or five groups. Limit the group size to six.

- Ask each group to find their own working space.

- Simultaneously the sculptors create an image of the problem as they see it.

- This is all done in silence. The sculptors do not verbally tell the people who or what they are in the sculpture.

It is up to the people sculpted to develop their own idea of what their role is in the image.

- When all three images are complete call for everyone to examine where they are in their image and identify their character and what their needs are.

- Call for everyone to speak their interior monologue out loud.

- Now the images will begin to move, still in silence, and each person, moving in slow motion, will move to get or achieve their needs or interests met.

- After a minute of that, call "Freeze."

- Now the images have changed, have everyone reassess where they are and what their needs are now.

- Call for interior monologues once more.

- Call for the images to move to get what their needs met. Move to achieve their goals.

- Call "Freeze."

- The images are again changed. Repeat the process several times.

Sometimes the images collide with one another and become mixed up. People's interpretations of what the image was about, what their characters' needs and interests were, and what they were supposed to do are often very different. This is an important point to make in the discussion portion of this exercise, during which everyone who wishes to can share their experience of the exercise. This is a powerful exercise that often stirs up a lot of emotions for people. By this time in the process, and through the use of group building and trust activities described in this book, the group should be comfortable enough to share emotional material.

CHAPTER 8

Creating the Dramatic Piece

We now move into the phase of the creation of a piece of theatre that represents the issue or conflict as it is. The piece of drama created will not seek to present the resolution of the conflict; instead it seeks to represent the problem itself, with all of the pieces and parts that have been explored in the previous sessions incorporated into the final presentation. This piece will then be used within the group or within the larger community or organization that the group is part of to create an interactive exploration of the possible actions that could transform the conflict into something positive.

Machine Sequence

The creation of the play begins with a series of exercises that I call the Machine Sequence. "Machines" is a standard, old theatre exercise that helps build creativity and group cohesion. Here it is used to explore ideas, emotions, and the problem the group is working on. Within the sequence is an exercise called Image Alive, which is not a traditional machine game, but has some of the same elements and it fits nicely in the sequence. This sequence can be used as a stand-alone technique for exploring an issue. It is fast paced and leads to a much clearer understanding of what the issue is and what feelings and words are associated with it.

 SIMPLE MACHINE

Begin with the Simple Machine. Ask if anyone in the group has done Machine before. Many people have played the game; it is used in many forums outside of theatre including schools and businesses.

- Everyone stands in a circle. It is important that everyone stands. When people sit they tend to lose their energy and drive to participate. I joke that all of the brain activity sinks to the bottom when people sit. Standing in a circle creates group energy and draws people into the action.

- Someone steps into the circle and begins a mechanical type motion that they repeat over and over again.

- Coach people to choose motions they can keep up for a long period of time, especially if the group is large.

- Another person then enters the circle and begins a motion that goes with or complements the motion of the first person.

- This continues until everyone who has a motion to add has done so.

- This first machine should be silent, after this sound can be added.

- During the second machine ask the group to find the sound of the machine.

- After three or four simple sound machines the group makes a machine that actually makes a product. The product can be real or imagined, something that is created by a machine or something that is not machine made. Many groups begin with trains and ice cream makers but they can move into more fun and inventive machines such as clouds and grass or they may get ahead of you and call for an emotion-making machine, which is the next step in the process.

❀ EMOTION MACHINE

- Use the same process as the simple machines only now the machines will produce emotions.

- Call on a wide range of emotions.

- Ask for people to think of the emotions they feel when they are involved in the problem the group is working on.

- Machine parts should enter with their sound.

- The sound can be a word, but it is better to keep it abstract and focus on the emotion and the sound it produces.

RELATIONSHIP COMPLETE THE IMAGE ALIVE

This exercise combines one of Boal's beginning image work exercises with character and relationship exploration. The result is often a powerful revelation of how characters involved in the conflict relate to each other physically in various settings and moments. This exercise combined with the following Issue Machine exercise launches points for the process of scene creation.

- Everyone chooses a partner, preferably someone they haven't spent a lot of time working with throughout the process. It is always good to have a mix of ideas and energies flowing around the room.
- The partners then choose a pair of characters from the character brainstorm list. They do not have to be characters that have a direct protagonist–antagonist relationship, but they should be characters that would be related to each other in some way.
- Everyone finds their own section of the space to be in with their partner. This exercise requires some space for the partners to move around and interact.
- As the exercise unfolds, partners may move far around the room and even apart from each other and then come together again.
- The partners begin by doing an exercise called Complete the Image.

- One partner strikes an image of their character doing something.

- The other partner looks at the image and then places their character in the image, completing the image.

- The first partner then unfreezes, steps back, and looks at the pose taken by their partner and then takes a new pose to create a totally different image.

- The image should be one that shows a possible action in the relationship between these two characters.

- After the partners go back and forth creating new and different images, call "Image Alive."

- The partners then can act out a scene that arises from the image and their relationship to each other.

- After a minute of this call "Freeze."

- One partner remains frozen and the other unfreezes, steps back, examines and re-enters the image to complete it.

- Continue with Complete the Image for a few more rounds and then again call "Image Alive."

- Continue the cycle of Complete the Image, Image Alive, Freeze for a few minutes.

Following this exercise people will want to talk about their experiences. However, it is important to keep the momentum and move into the last part of the machine sequence, then process the whole sequence.

❁ ISSUE MACHINE

This variation on the machine comes from the work of
Michael Rohd. It is a dynamic way to get the voices of the
characters and the words that need to be said about the
conflict all said at the same time.

- Everyone stands in a circle.

- Read the definition of the problem, the root causes,
  and the characters involved from the lists posted
  around the room.

- The group will now make a machine that produces
  the issue, problem, or conflict (however you wish to
  name it).

- As each person enters the machine they begin a
  mechanical motion, but instead of a sound they speak
  a word, phrase or sentence that is essential to the
  problem. They state this over and over again without
  changing it.

- Everyone in the group needs to enter the machine.

- As each person enters with their statement, move
  around the machine and jot down the words being said.

- When everyone has entered and the machine works
  as a whole for a few seconds, call "Freeze."

- Read the words heard in the machine.

- If it is a small group and there are more things that
  need to be said, the issue can be run through the
  machine a second time.

When the sequence is over it is time to debrief the activities. Begin by asking people's feelings simply about making a machine as a group. Then go into who people chose as characters in the Relationship Complete the Image Alive exercise. Ask each pair of partners to share their experience in that exercise. What was revealed about the characters' needs and relationships? Ask them to think about how that could be used in a scene.

Next review the Issue Machine and what people said and also what motions they chose. Which of the statements most need to be heard? Which words must be said in the performance for there to be a true exploration of the issue by the community?

CHAPTER 9

Play Making

The group is now ready to begin creating the piece of interactive theatre they will be performing.

Forum theatre: A brief description

The play they will make will be forum theatre. Here is how forum theatre works.

The play is designed to present people in situations of oppression, where they are confronted with conflict and either do not know what to do or the system around them keeps them from making a change. It should present the problem without giving the solutions. That is the role of the community or audience that views the show. That is the forum part of forum theatre. The play should make people in the audience want to shout out that this is wrong and the protagonist should do something else. They should be yelling, "Stop," which is just what you are going to ask them to do.

The play should be brief, about 10 to 15 minutes maximum. I have done three to five minute pieces that are very effective in the forum, especially if it is a single issue that everyone in the audience is aware of. It can be a play with a series of interrelated scenes or a series of vignettes designed to demonstrate the various aspects of the issue. Representational theatre, images, dance, music, all kinds of performing arts can be used. The group will decide what the best approach is.

When the play is ready to present, a community audience is gathered for a performance. The play is presented for the audience, who applaud at the end. Then the facilitator, called the Joker in TO language, steps out and begins a dialogue with the audience. There are some basic questions to ask the audience: Is what you just witnessed real? Can you see some part of yourself in the play? Is there something else the characters can do to change the situation? Should we try to change the situation?

Then the Joker invites the players to present the play again. Only this time, the audience is invited, urged, to yell "Stop" at any moment they see a character being oppressed or making a choice or non-choice that leads to perpetuation or worsening of the conflict. When they call for the stop, that audience member then comes on to the stage, takes the place of the oppressed or conflicted character and makes a change. The remaining actors in the scene stay and react in character to the intervention of the audience member. The idea is to make a theatre that is interactive, to transform the spectator into a "spectactor."

When the person finishes their intervention, the Joker asks them if they did what they wanted to do. They are given a very large round of applause, and the play goes on from where the intervention left off. A scene can be played multiple times with multiple interventions for the same scene. The play can have a new ending or the original ending can be played out, depending on the nature of the play and the interventions.

Once all of the interventions have been tried and the play is over, the dialogue and action-planning phase begins. This is covered in Chapter 11, Action Planning and Follow-up.

The playmaking phase is one that requires a great deal of trust and openness, so we begin with a group building, trust game. Then we move into improvisations of scene ideas group members have. Finally scenes are chosen, a story line expressed and the scenes are polished for presentation.

❀ FAINT BY NUMBERS

This is a fun and lively group trust exercise.

- Everyone begins to Cover the Space.

- Have small pieces of paper, each with a number written on it, from one to however many people are in the group, including the facilitator(s).

- Call "Freeze."

- Throw the papers down in the middle of the stage.

- Everyone comes and picks up a paper, reads the number to themselves and does not share what their number is.

- People begin to Cover the Space again.

- Instruct them that when the number on the paper they have is called they must faint.

- It is important that the faint is a very big, loud, dramatic faint, yelling loudly before beginning to fall.

This is everyone's chance to give their best, award-winning faint.

- When someone begins to faint, everyone in the group must come running to where that person is and catch them before they fall. Even if they are far from the person, they should move towards the person and provide support to the people who are doing the actual catching.

- Call out the numbers in order from one to the last number in the group.

- When everyone has fainted once, begin to call out numbers at random.

- Then begin to call out two numbers at once.

- Then three numbers.

- Finish by having everyone faint at once.

While people are moving around and fainting and catching people, make comments about how groups are like communities and they must work together to solve problems and help each other. Also, point out that sometimes problems come from unexpected sources and places and we must have tools to transform them. In this case it is our fellow group members, in other cases it is our co-workers, our families, our friends, and in the end it is our own selves.

❀ BEGINNING IMPROVISATIONS AND SCENE BUILDING

The group now begins to look at how they could present the issue in dramatic form.

- Begin by asking the group if anyone has ideas for scenes or story ideas.

- Following this discussion, ask who would like to set one of those scenes. They should indicate who is involved, where they are, and what they are doing.

- The actors placed in the scene improvise a scene between their characters.

- Following the first improvisation discuss what was strong, what elements need to be worked on, eliminated or if that scene will work in the play.

- Move to another scene or idea. Complete the above steps.

- If there is a larger group, you can divide them up and have them work on separate scenes together.

- The group will determine what the content of the play will be. It is the facilitator's job to ask questions that clarify what it is they wish to express about the conflict through this scene. Also, where are the points for intervention in the forum portion?

Once the beginning improvisations have happened, the group must make some final decisions about which scenes they will use, what story line will be utilized and who will play which roles.

Have everyone run their improvised scenes once more and have the whole group provide feedback.

While it may seem like a lot to ask of a group of non-actors to come up with a play from improvised scenes in just a few hours, it is amazing how the plays come together because the material is all there, written on a large piece of paper all around the room. The list of problems, the definition, the root causes, the characters, the stories, the words from the Issue Machine, they are all there for the participants to draw on. They also are people who are presenting an issue that is real in their lives, so if anything, there are often more ideas than can be done in a good piece of forum theatre.

One important aspect is that there needs to be in the scene a fairly clear protagonist and antagonist. As mentioned earlier, in a realistic presentation, these clear-cut lines are less and less clear, but it is important for there to be a character in the play the audience can relate to and want to change their behaviors. The antagonist should represent some of those root causes. In the forum play the audience will not be able to change the antagonist character. That is what is called magic. If only the people causing the problem would be different and nicer, then we could make the change. All of a sudden the heavy-handed boss who also sexually harasses all the young women is a caring understanding man who treats everyone with respect. That just doesn't happen in reality. So, the antagonist is not changeable. He or she can be changed only by the actions of the protagonist, i.e. the audience members and their interventions.

COP IN THE HEAD

Once some scenes with the protagonist(s) have been clarified the group can begin to explore some of the underlying, unspoken thoughts, fears and socio-cultural influences that keep people caught in conflicts and unable to transform their problems. These thoughts and fears and influences are the cops in the head.

This powerful technique comes from Augusto Boal. When Boal was in South America the structures and systems of power and oppression were pretty clear. Coercive forces oppressed people, the cop in the street, literally a cop with a gun to your head. However, when Boal was exiled in Europe, he saw people were still oppressed, that people still did not make choices that liberated themselves and those around them. But, now there was no cop with a gun. Instead, Boal surmised that the cops had become internalized and that now people had cops in the head.

This exercise is designed to determine the voices of society or the systems of oppression that keep people from changing and transforming their conflicts.

- Ask the person playing the protagonist to come forward.
- Place the person in a scene where they are confronted with one of the aspects of the issue.
- The protagonist has ideas for action to change the conflict, to overcome the oppression, yet he or she does not take the action.

- What are the voices or cops in the head of that person? Ask the protagonist actor first to choose someone from the group and place them in an image, a stance that shows what this voice looks like, and then to give them a short phrase to say.

- This person strikes the pose and states the phrase repeatedly while the person carries on the scene.

- The protagonist can have two or three cops.

- Solicit other members of the group for ideas for cops and what they are saying and look like.

- Play the scene with the cops in it this time. The cops are not real; they are part of the protagonist. They cannot change what they say. They can develop a repetitive motion that goes with their posture. They can move to follow the protagonist and keep their point being heard.

- Decide which cops are the most essential to be heard, which systematic constraints and voices need to be discussed.

- Then decide how to work the cops into the play. They can be in only one scene, they can always follow the protagonist everywhere he or she goes, or they can be there waiting to come out when they see a need to be heard. This depends on the nature of the play created.

Cops in the Head can also be done as an exercise with the group to examine various forces that keep us in patterns of behavior. For a full description of this technique, which is very rich and can be used in a variety of settings, see Augusto Boal's *The Rainbow of Desire* (2000).

Openings and closings

When the characters, story line, and cops in the head are in place, the scenes need to be placed in order. Once the scenes have an order and there is some kind of logical beginning, middle, and end, even if the scenes are unrelated, it is good to create either an opening or closing piece or both. Several methods are effective in creating these bookend pieces.

1. Open or close the show with an Issue Machine featuring the voices and characters that will be heard in the play.

2. Begin with an image of the characters and then have them come alive for a few seconds and then freeze.

3. End with one actor sculpting everyone in one representation of the problem that everyone has agreed to. This is very good for the forum, as audience members can come onstage and create a new sculpture that shows a different approach to the conflict, a vision of another future.

4. Begin or end with a song that is known by most of the audience that is related to the theme of the show.

5. A dance piece can be a good way to open or close, something simple in choreography, even popular music. One show we did had a whole theme of salsa dancing and after the forum, was over everyone in the audience danced.

This is by no means an exhaustive list of possible openings or closings, but it gives you an idea as to what you could do. The group will find the right piece for them, the facilitator's job is to coach, push, and encourage them with ideas, support, and constructive direction.

Rehearsal

Because the play will be unscripted and largely improvised it is important to rehearse it several times before going before the community with it. I suggest that at least three run-throughs, from start to finish, is best. Because it is an unwritten script there need to be key words or actions that cue scene changes. There are elements to each scene that are essential and these "beats" must be hit if the play is to move with any kind of aesthetic. Use these run-throughs to synchronize the beats and get everyone to meet their cues. The group members will be nervous about forgetting what to say, that is why it is important to have key words that lead to transitions and important messages being delivered.

Practice forum

When the play is all ready (though it may not appear so, you must let go and trust that the importance lies in the message and the creation of dialogue) an important step is allowing the group a chance to practice working in the forum theatre style.

- Choose one of the scenes from the play, one that people feel most comfortable with their characters in and/or one that has a lot of energy around it.
- Have the scene performed.
- Re-present the scene this time inviting other members of the group who are not in the scene to call "Stop" when they feel they have an intervention.
- The actors who are not replaced should respond to the intervention as their character. It is important to explore how this character would react to such an

intervention. What are the needs and interests and positions of this character?

- Repeat this for as many people as have interventions.
- Try it with other scenes so that everyone can have an experience in the forum environment before going to the community. Sometimes time does not permit this, but doing some forum practice is really important for the group to see how it works.

A word about technical design

While costumes, props, sound, and lighting can certainly add to the overall aesthetic of the piece you create, always remember that the content is what is most important here. Another thing to remember is that if one is dependent on sets, lights, costumes or anything else, there is always the chance that these things may fail you.

Overall, I try to keep props, costumes, and set pieces to a minimum. It makes for fewer things to remember and therefore fewer things to forget. Sometimes just a hat or a jacket is all one needs to represent the intended character. Don't get bogged down in the costumes. Usually, because these stories come from the lives of the people themselves, they have the costumes and props needed in their homes or workplaces. Lights and sound are something that if you have the luxury of having them available use them by all means. However, this type of theatre is one that is designed to create dialogue and break down the fourth wall of theatre, that imaginary divider between the stage and audience. By limiting the technical aspects of the performance, you create a less intimidating, more inviting space for the community to enter with their interventions.

CHAPTER 10

Presentation

The process culminates with the community performance. This can take many forms. If the group is part of a business or organization, then it is good to have a presentation for the rest of the organization. If it is a community-based group, then a presentation at a community center is in order. A university or high school student should present before their peers. And, if it is a group drawing from all sectors and age groups, then a public performance at a central location can be used to generate dialogue within the community as a whole.

Once you have your location set, ensure that the group has had a chance to practice the play in the space. It is optimal to have the performance space be where the preparation has taken place, but this is not always possible. If that is the case, schedule in some time prior to the performance time for a run-through of the play in the space.

When the community audience is all seated, it is important for the facilitator/Joker to come out and "warm up" the crowd. It is especially important to involve the audience physically and emotionally right from the start, because later you are going to ask them to get out of their seats and go onstage.

Here is one example of how to warm up an audience for a forum theatre presentation.

- Begin with a brief description of the process and how the play they are about to see was created.

- Ask if anyone has participated in an interactive theatre performance before.

- Ask if there are any professional actors in the audience (usually no one will raise their hand, maybe one person).

- Then ask the cast if any of them are professional actors (usually no one will raise their hand, maybe one person). This helps establish that no one here is a professional actor; instead we are using theatre, a very old form of communication, as a vehicle for community dialogue. It is a way to transform conflicts.

- Ask if anyone in the audience has ever acted before. Again, almost no one will raise his or her hand. Ask them to think back to when they were in Kindergarten or First Grade and they played the tree in the school Christmas pageant. Most everyone will then raise their hands.

- Now, ask everyone to stand up.

- Ask the audience to create a statue or image with their body when they hear a word that you call out.

- Call out words like Love, Peace, Hate, and some words related to the topic being discussed in the play.

- Ask everyone to sit down.

- Explain how forum theatre works, that we will watch the play once, and then it will be presented a second time during which anyone can call "Stop" and come into the scene and try something different to change the conflict.
- Begin the show.

When the first run-through is finished and everyone applauds, the facilitato/Joker steps out onto the stage and asks the questions: Is what you just witnessed real? Can you see some part of yourself in the play? Is there something else the characters can do to change the situation? Should we try to change the situation? We hope that the audience will answer, "Yes" to all of these questions. Then have the audience practice clapping and yelling "Stop" all together. When they do it loudly twice, begin the play a second time.

This time the Joker stays close by the stage and watches the crowd closely to see if someone is ready to call stop. Sometimes the Joker can make eye contact and encourage someone who wants to come in but is hesitant. You never want to force people, but some body language and eye contact may be all some people need. The first intervention is always the one that breaks the ice and after that, and people see that the interventionist survives and even had positive results, people are more open to entering with their idea.

Run the forum as described above, allowing people to try interventions. Some audience members may wish to come in several times throughout. Repeat spectactors are fine, but be sensitive to the need for everyone to try out their idea.

As each intervention is completed, take a moment to define the intervention in a few words with the audience.

Write the intervention down on a large piece of paper somewhere in view of everyone in the room. At the end of the forum portion of the play, you will have a list of the interventions tried.

When the play has ended a second time and applause and bows are over, ask the audience to take a moment and think about the play, how the issue presented is played out in their own lives, and what they might do differently tomorrow based upon what has happened today. After a minute or two in silence, ask them to then share with their neighbor one thing that they commit to doing individually to change the problem presented in the play.

CHAPTER 11

Action Planning and Follow-up

Boal has called the actions in the forum, "rehearsal for real life." Dramatic Problem Solving takes those rehearsals and provides support to individuals and groups to make them real. This is done through concrete action planning and follow-up.

 CREATING THE ACTION PLAN

When everyone has done their interventions, a discussion of the forum has concluded, and everyone has committed to one action they will take or a behavior they will change, the group is ready to make an action plan.

The plan is designed to cover a time frame of one to three months. People should work on actions that have short-term outcomes and long-term impact.

On a large sheet of paper write down the following categories:

Problem addressed	What action	Goal	Who	When	First meeting	First check-in

- Review the interventions and the commitments from the audience and ask what actions the group would like to work on collaboratively.

- As ideas come up ask first, what part of the problem that intervention addresses. Naming the problem is important.

- Then ask what the concrete action will be.

- Name one or two goals of the action; this is something that the small group that commits to the action can flesh out more in their first meeting.

- Define when the action will begin and end, tentatively.

- Then a very important step is to arrange a time for the first meeting of the action takers. This is so crucial if something is actually going to happen. People have a tendency to talk about what should be done, the great actions that would help change a problem, but normally do not commit to a time to devote to that action. By making a first meeting and getting people to commit to attending, the first step is taken towards concretizing the interventions and their results.

- A time for a first check-in as to the results of the action is important to set a deadline for some kind of action.

While the problems groups are confronting are often very large and systemic in nature, the action plan can highlight small things as well as big things the group can do to change that system. It is only through a series of small steps that we can begin to make changes.

Follow-up

The facilitator's role is not to attend every action plan follow-up meeting. The idea is that people will be working on their issues in the way they see fit. The facilitator can call and check in with those who have committed to the action plan to see how they are doing. Perhaps they need you to come and facilitate one of their sessions and help them clarify their goals and action steps.

When the date for their first check-in comes up, the facilitator can either arrange a meeting or do a phone or email check-in. Ask questions about what has been done, what is planned, and how many times has the group met or completed an action since the presentation. Keep notes for use in the community action plan review phase.

 COMMUNITY ACTION PLAN REVIEW

After three months, the community is ready to review their action plan. This is done through an interactive session open to the original group members, the community presentation audience members, and anyone who has subsequently been involved in the action plan.

This session utilizes a lot of image theatre to look at what happened, what worked, what did not work, and what can and will be done next.

- Begin with some kind of warm-up activity taken from the Warm-ups section of the book (Chapter 12).

- Verbally review the action plan.

- Ask each person or group that was involved in the action plan to come forward and present a summary of their action.

- This is not a verbal summary, but a summary through images.

- The person or group will, using themselves and as many members of the group as they need, create three images.

- Image 1 will show the problem they were responding to as it was.

- Image 2 will show the action(s) they took, showing both the successes and failures of the interventions.

- Image 3 will show the problem as it is today, demonstrating the areas they still identify as needing transformation.

- Hold a group discussion and then ask anyone to come and create an image that shows a possible action or intervention to transform the conflict as it is today.

- Do this for as many people as want to come up with an intervention.

- Review and evaluate which options are most feasible and doable.

- Add these to the new action plan, posted on a large piece of paper on the wall, using the same format and columns as the original action plan.

- Repeat the cycle for all of the original action plan steps.

- At the end of the session, a new action plan has been created and the group is ready to continue on with the transformation of their community or organization, as well as themselves.

At this point the group, community, or organization should be ready to carry on the work on their own. The original group members have the experience and facilitation skills now to analyze and develop new plans of action. The long-term goal of the process is to leave a group of people behind with a set of new skills for conflict analysis and transformation that they can utilize in all aspects of their lives.

CHAPTER 12

Warm-ups

Throughout the process it is important to have exercises designed to warm up the group, to activate them. This is best done by activities that move the body while activating the mind's creativity. Below are some warm-ups that can be used at the start of sessions, after a break, and to bridge from one phase to another, especially if people have been sitting and talking for a while.

 CAT AND MOUSE

This is a game of tag that gets everyone moving. It also involves creative expression with your body and quick thinking.

- Ask for two volunteers. One will be a cat and the other a mouse.

- Everyone else forms partnerships and the partners link arms.

- The partners spread around the space.

- The cat begins to chase the mouse.
- If the mouse is tagged, the roles reverse and the mouse becomes something larger than the cat and begins to chase the cat.
- The person being chased can link arms with one of the partners.
- This causes the partner on the opposite side to pop off.
- The person who pops off then begins to chase the other player, acting like something larger than he or she is.
- The play continues like this, back and forth, linking arms and popping off.
- This is a game the facilitator can play as well.
- It is important to stress the full, big physical expression of the animal or whatever role you take on to chase your prey.
- You can call for movement that is only walking, slow motion, crawling, super speed, anything that will get people in touch with their bodies and physical expression.

 FREEZE TAG

This is a traditional improvisational theatre warm-up. It is especially helpful as a warm-up before a performance or before going into improvisational scene building. The key things to stress here are the need for: big choices, acceptance, and clear communication.

- Ask for two volunteers.

- Everyone else stands or sits, ready to enter the scene.

- The two people ask the group for a situation for them to act out.

- They begin acting out the scene, using big choices and big physical gestures.

- The rest of the group is coached to look for moments where the action physically looks and reminds them of something else.

- At any point someone from the group calls "Freeze."

- The players freeze and the person who called freeze enters the scene.

- That person takes the place of one of the players, assuming their physical position.

- They then begin a totally different scene, doing something totally different.

- The important thing is that their choice must be justified by the physical position they took. For example, if in the scene before the players were holding a fire hose together, when the person comes in and assumes the position of holding a fire hose they must change what they are holding, use that position, change it to, for example wrestling a large python, and move on with their scene. They cannot just walk in and make the object in their hands magically disappear.

- This game is best when it is fast moving, with many people calling freeze. Scenes that go on for more than 15 seconds tend to run out of energy.

- When you finish playing the exercise for the first item with the group, discuss how it was for people. Ask how they felt with the quick thinking, fast action of the exercise. Some people love Freeze Tag and others do not. Everyone loves to watch, but not everyone will join in. Encourage them to look at why and to try next time to get in and try something.

 ## BOXING/LOVING

This warm-up gets people in touch with the ways they can move and the ways they can express themselves. It is also an interesting social study because normally people can come up with many more ways to hurt each other than to love each other.

- Divide the group into pairs.

- Each partner stands 10 to 15 feet apart from the other.

- They begin by having a fight or boxing match from this distance.

- The goal is to clearly deliver messages and accept them in the biggest way possible.

- Partners take turns sending and receiving the punches, kicks, or whatever other motions they can think of to fight their partner.

- After a few minutes of fighting, have the partners stop.

- Now ask them to change from boxing to loving.

- Still staying 10 to 15 feet away, how can they show love and affection in many different ways and how can they receive the messages with their whole body?

 COMPLETE THE IMAGE

This is an exercise that simultaneously warms up the body and prepares people for doing image theatre work. It is useful at any point in the process, but especially before doing a lot of image work.

- Ask everyone to find a partner.

- Everyone finds their own section of the space to be in with their partner. This exercise requires some space for the partners to move around and interact. As the exercise unfolds partners may move far around the room and even apart from each other and then come together again.

- One partner strikes an image, a frozen statue.

- The other partner looks at the image and then places themselves physically in relation to their partner, thus completing the image.

- The first partner then unfreezes, steps back, and looks at the pose taken by their partner and then takes a new pose to create a totally different image.

- This back and forth continues for several minutes.

- Encourage the partners to use their whole bodies, to explore different ways to be in relation to the other.

- Continue for a few minutes and then have everyone freeze in their last image. One by one have the partners unfreeze and observe everyone else in the room in their final images.

 CARNIVAL IN RIO

This Boal exercise is a great exploration of group decision-making. I use this with groups of students who are learning how to use consensus decision-making. It is also a great warm-up activity that can sometimes last a long while as the people come together in their dance. This exercise can be very revelatory in terms of group cohesion, strong individual personalities, leaders in the group, and conflict resolution styles.

- Have the group divide up into groups of three.

- In each group decide who will be A, B, and C.

- Everyone begins by simultaneously creating their own sound and movement dance, something they can do repeatedly and can be easily copied.

- When everyone has one, the group members take turns demonstrating their dance to their partners. The other group members try to replicate the dance of each partner.

- When everyone has demonstrated their dance to the others in their group they must all begin their individual dance again.

- After a few seconds of the simultaneous individual dances, each group must find a way to create a sound-movement dance from the three individual dances. This is all done without the use of words.

- Once each group forms their own, unique dance incorporating all three individual dances, the groups all go out to observe and dance with the other groups.

- All of the groups, working as individuals or groups must then begin to change their dances to one community sound-movement dance. The sound is important; this is not just a dance but also a sound exercise.

- The group must communicate non-verbally to create a new community dance.

- The exercise ends when the group is all doing the same sound-movement.

- Coach the group to make sure that they are happy with the dance the community is doing; do not just go along. If you feel that a piece is important, fight for it.

- This is an exercise in consensus building. However, forming consensus does not mean you have to just give up your ideas and go along with the crowd. In fact, the point of consensus is to include every voice, even the smallest minority, in the decision-making process equally.

- The time it takes to form the community dance and the way it happens will be very indicative of how the group works. You can see which people are accommodators and which are more assertive. If it is a group of people who know each other well, sometimes they will all do a dance that is already known to the group. Some groups will come to consensus quickly because they are good task doers and want to achieve the desired goal. All of these can be points for questioning and discussion when the exercise finishes.

 ## 2 ×3 × BRADFORD

This is a warm-up that comes from Boal and is a very good introduction to the challenges of remembering dialogue and following cues. It is an exercise that seems simple, but is often mentally challenging for people. Encourage everyone to be big with their body motions and sounds.

- Have everyone choose a partner. If there is an odd number, the facilitator can play, too.
- The partners will be counting together in this fashion.

    Partner A: One.

    Partner B: Two.

    Partner A: Three.

    Partner B: One.

    Partner A: Two.

    Partner B: Three.

    Partner A: One.

    And so on.

- When they all have accomplished this feat, they will now incorporate the sound and movement piece. It is good to demonstrate with someone. The sound and movement counting goes like this:

  Partner A: One.

  Partner B: Two.

  Partner A: Three.

  Partner B: One.

  Partner A: Two.

  Partner B: Three.

  Partner A: First sound and movement (an invented sound and body movement).

  Partner B: Two.

  Partner A: Three.

  Partner B: First sound and movement (same as the one above).

  Partner A: Two.

  Partner B: Three.

  Partner A: First sound and movement.

  Partner B: Second sound and movement (another, different invented sound and body movement).

  Partner A: Three.

  Partner B: First sound and movement.

  Partner A: Second sound and movement.

  Partner B: Three.

  Partner A: First sound and movement.

Partner B: Second sound and movement.

Partner A: Third sound and movement (another, different invented sound and body movement).

Partner B: First sound and body movement.

Partner A: Second sound and body movement.

Partner B: Third sound and body movement.

Partner A: First sound and body movement.

Partner B: Second sound and body movement.

Partner A: Third sound and body movement.

And so on.

- The object is to get out of what we are used to being the order of things and begin to think and remember different, new information. Quick thinking, cooperation, and physical expression are all important aspects of this exercise.

 SQUIRRELS

This is a fun game taken from the Children's Creative Conflict Resolution program and taught to me by the wonderful Celina Garcia.

- Everyone forms groups of three. There should be one or two people left out. They will be the leaders. If there is a perfect split into groups of three, the facilitator can play.

- Each group decides who will be one of three roles: door, window, or squirrel.

- The door and window use their outstretched arms to form a house for the squirrel. The squirrel goes inside the house.

- The leader, outside of the houses, then calls out window, door, squirrel, or earthquake.

- If they call window, then all of the windows must change houses and the leader seeks to become a window in one of the houses. The same applies if the leader calls doors, or squirrels.

- If the leader calls earthquake, then everyone must change and form new houses with squirrels in them.

- It is important to instruct the group that when the earthquake is called everyone loses their identity and can become anything they want or need to be to meet their need of forming a new trio. Sometimes people will be not join a house that needs a window because they can't let go of their original identity. They say, "but I'm a squirrel."

- Continue changing leaders for a few minutes.

- Ask the group how the game made them feel and how they think it is or is not relevant to their lives.

 ## THE GREAT WIND BLOWS

This is a great game for getting to know the group. It helps people realize what they have in common beyond what they see from the outside.

- Everyone sits in chairs in a circle with the facilitator standing in the middle.

- The facilitator calls out, "The Great Wind Blows for anyone who…" and says something about himself or herself. This can be a physical trait, an experience, a belief, anything.

- Anyone in the group for whom that is also true for must get up and find another chair in the circle.

- The facilitator tries to find a chair, thus leaving one extra person left in the middle to be the leader and call out for whom The Great Wind Blows.

- Continue like this for several rounds until everyone or most everyone has had a chance to be in the center.

- This is a great game to get people moving and to get to know people better.

- Sometimes people only call out physical traits, such as anyone who is wearing blue or sandals or earrings. Try to encourage the participants to call out qualities, likes and dislikes, experiences, things we cannot see or know just from the outside.

 LABOR DANCE

This is a game I learned from Marc Weinblatt in Washington. It is a great way to get people thinking about creative ways to express their everyday lives.

- Everyone begins to Cover the Space.

- Ask the participants to think about an activity, some kind of labor that they do on a regular basis.

- Ask them to begin to act as if they were doing that task.

- After a few seconds of them miming their labor, call them to begin to change their labor into a dance.

- The dance can be ballet, modern, tap, representational, or realistic.

- Encourage them to go for their dance, to really transform their labor into art.

- Have them develop a finale for their dance.

- When everyone has finished their dance have everyone come together in a circle.

- Invite anyone who would like to come into the center of the circle and share their dance with the group.

- If anyone in the group feels that they recognize this labor, they should enter the circle and begin doing their own dance version of that work.

- When everyone that wants to join in has done so ask them all to finish with a big finale.

- After a big applause, ask each person who entered with their own dance what labor they were doing.

- Finally ask the original dancer what their labor was.

- Repeat this for as many different people as wish to share their labor dance.

 PUSHING

This physical warm-up is a good exercise to demonstrate the need for give and take for there to be dramatic tension in a scene. It is also good preparation for the forum performance, centering on give and take of energies, not overpowering someone just because you can but also not caving in to very strong energy.

- Everyone chooses a partner.
- The partners stand facing each other.
- Each person places their hands on the shoulders of their partner.
- They both begin pushing each other.
- The goal is not to win a pushing match nor to find perfect balance, but to keep pushing back and forth, maintaining visible tension between the partners.
- Encourage the partners to avoid dancing with their partner, as some people will do, but to look for different and surprising ways they can push their partner.
- After a minute or so of the shoulder pushing have the partners stop.
- The partners now stand back to back with their backs touching.
- They begin pushing each other with their backs.
- Again, they should be looking for tension and give and take.

- Especially in the back-to-back portion it is good to point out the mutual dependence and trust there is in their relationship.

- When they have pushed back to back for a minute have them stop.

- The third and final pushing will be bottom to bottom.

- This is a very funny twist on pushing but at the same time it is a good physical warm-up.

- The partners, depending on their height, weight, and physical strength differences or similarities, must find out variations and adaptations for this exercise.

 THREE IRISH DUELS

This is a Boal warm-up that really gets the blood pumping. The Irish part becomes apparent in the second part of the exercise.

- First have everyone choose a partner.

- The partners begin with Duel 1 – Knees.

- The object is simply to touch the knees of the other person while not allowing them to touch your knees. You can use your hands to block the other person.

- Next is Duel 2 – Feet.

- The object is to touch the other person's foot with your foot while always maintaining one foot in the air. This quickly begins to resemble Irish step dancing, only not nearly so graceful and much funnier. (Make sure everyone either has shoes on or no shoes at all; a mix of either will lead to injured toes.)

- Finally, the partners complete Duel 3 – Finger Swords.

- Both players place their hand on their lower back with the palm facing upwards.

- The object is to touch the open hand on the back with your finger (sword) while not letting your partner touch your open palm.

- This exercise is mainly a physical warm-up and is very good to use when the group seems to be losing energy or just coming back from lunch.

✿ DANCING AND SINGING

Dancing and singing in a group, any song that everyone knows or a simple one that is lively and can incorporate a simple rhythmic movement makes a good warm-up. Drumming and dancing or playing a CD of African or Irish or any other lively dance music will get the group going. The facilitator should take the lead and set the tone for a lively dance. Sing out and encourage singing out. Any group circle dances like those done in Dances for Universal Peace are very good, especially the more lively ones such as, "Wearing My Long Tail Feathers" or "Out Beyond Ideas."

 MINIMUM SURFACE CONTACT

This is an exercise that begins as an individual physical warm-up and ends as a group building, and trust building exercise.

- Everyone begins to Cover the Space.

- As they move they begin to discover and play with how they can continue to move and maintain the minimum amount of contact between their body and the floor.

- They need to keep moving and get away from only having contact with the floor through their feet.

- Perhaps they will be touching only one knee and one hand, slowly moving towards just their shoulder blades touching.

- This becomes a moving exploration of the different ways you can be connected to the ground.

- After a minute ask everyone to find another person, continuing to be in minimum surface contact.

- With their partner they must explore how they can work together to both maintain the minimum surface contact.

- After a minute of that have each partnership find another duo.

- The four people must work together to maintain minimum contact between themselves and the floor.

- After four, continue doubling the group size until the entire group is working to find the minimum surface contact of the whole group.

- Some people, especially the smaller and lightweight ones, may find themselves in the air for a good portion of this exercise. Others may be called on to do a good deal of the lifting and support work.

 EL GALLO VIUDO

This is a version of a game that comes from El Salvador. It is a fun way to practice non-verbal communication and focused attention.

- The group stands in two concentric circles.

- The people in the inner circle all stand in front of someone in the outer circle.

- There should be one person in the outer circle without anyone standing in front of him or her.

- This person is the *Gallo Viudo*, which means Widower Rooster.

- The Gallo Viudo wants to get a new hen to be his wife.

- He must use non-verbal communication to get one of the hens, those in the inner circle, to leave their place and come and stand in front of him.

- The roosters in the outer circle must stand with their hands behind their backs.

- When the rooster sees his hen leaving he must grab her before she goes. If he does not, then he becomes the Gallo Viudo.

- The game continues on like this, with people leaving their spots; some being caught and some getting away.

- After a few minutes, have the two circles switch so that everyone can have the experience of being the Gallo and the hen.

 MIRRORS

This is a classic improvisational theatre exercise. For the best example of it see Groucho Marx in "Animal Crackers."

- Everyone chooses a partner.

- The partners decide who will be the person and who the mirror.

- The person begins to do things.

- The mirror attempts to match the motions of the person at the same time they are being done, creating a mirror image.

- This is an exercise in non-verbal communication, anticipation, acceptance, and physicality.

- Encourage big gestures from the people looking at the mirror.

- After a few minutes have the partners switch roles.

- Finally, have the partners begin acting in mirror form.

- Their goal is to work so that both are the person and both are the mirror, such that if an audience were to watch them they would not be able to tell who was leading and who was following.

There are hundreds more warm-up activities. This is a list of a few I rely on during the process. You can use any other warm-up games or activities that you know. There are many more great theatre games in Boal's *Games for Actors and Non-Actors* (2002) as well as Viola Spolin's *Improvisation for the Theatre* (1963).

Another good thing to try is to ask if someone in the group would like to lead a warm-up exercise; something they have done or led in the past that they think would be good for the group.

CHAPTER 13

Closing Exercises

When you have finished a session, it is important to close with an exercise that brings the group together. This can be a verbal or physical exercise. It should be something brief. It should avoid open-endedness, for example just sitting down at the end of the session and saying, "OK, let's talk about today." The goal is that the process itself will bring out all that needs to be said and provide space for people to speak about their experience in the moment. They should not have to wait until the end of the session to share.

The following exercises bring closure to the session. The Appreciation Circle is one I always use at the end of the process.

 MASSAGE

Everyone loves to get a massage. This group massage exercise is always a favorite.

- Everyone, including the facilitator, stands in a tight circle – standing shoulder to shoulder.

- Everyone turns 90 degrees to the right.

- They then give the person in front of them a neck massage.

- After a few minutes, everyone turns 180 degrees to the left and gives a massage to the person in front of them, thanking that person for the massage they just received.

- Close with everyone facing center for a moment of silence.

 GLASS COBRA

This is a blind exercise that works on trust and teamwork. The facilitator leads this from the outside.

- Everyone stands in a tight circle, shoulder to shoulder.

- Everyone closes their eyes.

- Everyone turns 90 degrees to the right.

- Everyone then begins to study the neck and shoulders of the person in front of them with their hands.

- While that happens begin to tell the following story:

- "Once, many years ago, there lived a beautiful cobra. This cobra was extraordinary because it was made of glass. It was very beautiful and when the sun shone upon it all the colors of the rainbow radiated from it. One day the cobra was climbing high on a tree. As it slithered out onto a high branch, a strong wind came unexpectedly and blew the cobra off of the branch. When it fell to the ground it shattered into many pieces which were then picked up and carried by the wind all around the world."

- Everyone lets go of the person in front of them and begins to move around the room with their eyes closed, totally in silence.

- Continue with the story: "The pieces of the glass cobra were carried all over the world, to Africa, Asia, America, Europe (here you can add in the places the people in the group are from as well, which you learned in the opening Sociometry exercise). Over the years the pieces continued to be carried around the world. One day something miraculous occurred and all of the pieces were together again for the first time. They were carried all together to (wherever you are that day). The cobra began to put itself back together."

- Everyone continues with their eyes closed. But now they search with their hands for the neck and shoulders that was in front of them when the cobra was whole.

- When someone finds the correct neck and shoulders they should stop and hold on to that person.

- The group continues searching until the whole circle has been reunited. When the circle has been reunited, close the story by saying, "And when the cobra was reunited it transformed from glass into steel and could never be broken again."

- When the circle is re-formed have everyone open their eyes.

- Check to see if the Glass Cobra was put back together correctly.

- End with everyone facing center, holding hands for a moment of collective smiling.

Silence

Sometimes people are very emotionally and physically charged at the end of the session. Having everyone sit in silence for five or even ten minutes can help everyone center, focus, and collect their thoughts before they go on to their life outside of the group.

 JOE EGG OR TRUST CIRCLE

This is the classic trust exercise that is used in virtually all group-building workshops.

- Everyone stands in a very tight circle. The diameter of the circle should be no more than the height of one person. If you are working with a large group, divide them into groups of 10 to 12.

- One person steps into the center of the circle.

- That person closes their eyes and crosses their arms in front of them.

- They then fall either forward or backward, keeping their body stiff and their feet together.

- The people in the circle stand with their hands in front of them and their knees bent.

- Working together, the group catches the falling person and passes them around the circle.

- The group can pass them around the circle, across the circle, or a combination of these.

- The most important thing is that the person in the middle allows themselves to fall and be caught.

- After a few seconds of falling in the circle, stop the person and ask them to open their eyes.

- Repeat this for everyone in the circle. If someone does not want to do the exercise, it is OK, but ask them to examine why they do not want to within themselves. Always ask people to push themselves beyond their comfort zone, but never force anyone to do something.

 ONE WORD

This closing circle exercise wraps up the session with a verbal reflection. But by limiting everyone to saying only one word it keeps it brief. It also makes for a powerful, often poetic ending to a session. It is especially good after an intense emotional session or where a lot was accomplished.

- Everyone sits or stands in a circle.

- Ask people to think of one word to end the session. The word can be related to any of the following prompts: What are you feeling right now? What will you take from today's session? What is something you learned today? What is a goal for you now, after today's work? Or any other prompt that you feel is good for the group in that moment.

- End with a moment of silence.

- The facilitator can write down the words on a sheet of small or large paper and read back the word list when everyone has shared.

 VOCAL CRESCENDO

This is a group vocal exercise that, when it works and everyone is listening to each other, is very moving.

- Everyone stands in a small circle, shoulder to shoulder.

- Everyone begins singing or humming a soft, low note, singing in a range they are comfortable in. This is a vocal exercise and non-singers should not worry about how they sound.

- The group begins to raise the volume on their note.

- The notes get louder and louder until everyone is singing as loudly as possible.

- When the crescendo is reached, the group slowly brings the note back down to the starting level.

- Stand in silence with eyes closed and feel the energy in the circle and throughout the group.

APPRECIATION CIRCLE

This circle exercise is a great way to close the whole process. It is usually done either the afternoon before the performance or the day after the first community performance.

- Everyone sits in a circle.
- The person to the left or right of the facilitator begins and thanks and says words of appreciation to the group. They can say things about everyone individually, or to just some people specifically. Leave it very open ended.
- The appreciations continue around the circle until they come back to the facilitator.
- The facilitator then shares their appreciations and thankfulness to each member of the group.
- Close with a minute or two of silence.

There are many other closing activities you can use with your groups. The most important thing is to give closure to each session.

CHAPTER 14

Applications

Case Study of DPS in Costa Rica

The DPS process was given its fullest implementation during a project in the San Jose, Costa Rica neighborhood known as La Carpio. This burgeoning squatter's community of 35,000 people, mainly immigrants from Nicaragua and their children, lies on the outskirts of the city, right next to the largest active landfill in Costa Rica. Here, working with a group of women dedicated to making change in their community, we undertook the DPS process.

DPS was brought into La Carpio via the work of the Costa Rican Humanitarian Foundation (CRHF). This NGO has been working with the people, especially the women and children, of La Carpio to bring them basic education, health care, and self-development actions. A group of women working at a day care center sponsored by the CRHF were invited to take part in a group process designed to transform some conflicts from their community. The group of women moved through the steps outlined in this book, generating knowledge about their own lives and their community.

The women were single mothers who had been living in this poor neighborhood for several years. Some of them, like Marlene, lived in one-room shacks on the edge of a sometimes raging river at the bottom of a hill that cascaded mud and trash. Others were mothers supporting several small children, eking out a living in this harsh environment. However, in spite of these conditions, the women were positive and committed to working to improve and change the future for themselves and their children.

We completed the exercises, the warm-ups and icebreakers, the trust and group-building activities, we listened to each other's stories, unpacked them, created images, and in the end created a play about an issue of central concern to the community – trash. Through a forum theatre event the community identified several concrete actions that could be taken to improve the trash problem in their community in the short, medium, and long term. An action plan was created via facilitated dialogue. These actions were implemented successfully and a change was noted in the daily life of the community members. Chief among the change was in the attitude and self-esteem of the participants in the workshop.

Emboldened by this new sense of power and the success of the process, the women decided that they would like to continue using DPS as a way of solving their problems. The CRHF had an idea that they could focus on a heath issue. The topic of breast cancer awareness was chosen for two reasons. One is that this is an important issue for all women and the level of education is low. Second was that there is a specific group of women in Costa Rica who are at high risk of breast cancer. These are agricultural plantation workers, especially coffee plantations. The women living in La Carpio had all been seasonal, migrant coffee pickers at one point in their lives. Some still did it during the season. They knew first hand the isolation and lack of health resources there are at the plantations. For these reasons the Foundation and the women decided to use DPS to examine the issue of breast cancer and bring an interactive theatre play to the plantations to create action-based dialogue with the migrant workers there.

Through stories and images created in workshop, the group created a play about the reasons behind the lack of health education and breast cancer awareness. The play, entitled the Coffee Dance, shared the life story of so many young women who make choices based on immediate need and lack of opportunity that in the end lead to ignorance about important issues, like breast cancer, and eventually poor health. The women worked to apply for a grant to take the play to a wider community. The Susan G. Komen for the Cure Foundation gave a grant to develop and tour the play. This play was taken around the country and presented at coffee plantations where risks for breast cancer are high and health education is low. The play was presented in conjunction with a mobile clinic provided by the CRHF to give free health screenings and information about breast cancer. Hundreds of people saw the play. They engaged in dialogues. They received valuable health information and perhaps they rehearsed for a new life.

Following this, the group decided that they wanted to look again at their own community. However, this time they were ready to take on the whole process by themselves. They took the DPS model and worked on creating a play that tells the story of their lives and the lives of so many of the marginalized urban poor. They are calling it "The Dignity of Poverty." They use the play, along with the other two, to give a name to the face, a story to the picture that is seen by many volunteers who come to La Carpio via the CRHF and other organizations.

This whole process was a demonstration of how DPS and theatre can create the space where people can become empowered to think about old problems in new ways and with a new self-image work to help themselves and others.

Conclusion

When this process works well there are moments where profound change can happen. The changes are realized on many levels. People find and explore places they did not know they had or had left covered for a long time. New ways of seeing and thinking about an old problem lead to new ways of dealing with the issue. Organizations can adopt new strategies, people new lifestyles, and groups new directions. I have seen all of these things happen.

I hope that everyone using this process will make it their own and modify it to meet the needs of the groups they work with. In the true tradition of Freire and Boal, the change must be named, brought to the level of consciousization, and changed by the people where they are and to the point they are capable of. All the resources we need for revolutionary change to the systems of oppression can be found within our own communities, groups, and organizations. It does not have to come from outside experts and consultants. In fact, the changes will be more real and long lasting if they come from within and are implemented from within.

Bibliography

Below is a list of works I have used to compile this book and the process it describes. Some are cited within the text and others are works I have used as guides for the work.

Boal, A. (1975) *200 Ejercicios y Juegos Para el Actor y Para el no Actor con Ganas de Decir Algo a Traves Del Teatro*. Buenos Aires: Crisis.

Boal, A. (1978) *Theatre of the Oppressed*. New York: Theatre Communications Group.

Boal, A. (1998) *Legislative Theatre*. New York: Routledge.

Boal, A. (2000) *The Rainbow of Desire*. New York: Routledge.

Boal, A. (2002) *Games for Actors and Non-Actors*. New York: Routledge.

Broome, B. (1998) "Overview of conflict resolution activities in Cyprus: Their contribution to the peace process." *The Cyprus Review 10*, 1, 47–66.

Cohen Cruz, J. and Schutzman, M. (eds) (2006) *A Boal Companion: Dialogues on Theatre and Cultural Politics*. London: Routledge.

Cossa, M., Ember, S., Grover, L. and Hazelwood, J. (1996) *Acting Out: The Workbook, A Guide to the Development and Presentation of Issue-Oriented, Audience-Interactive, Improvisational Theatre*. New York: Brunner/Routledge.

Dayton, T. (1990) *Drama Games: Techniques for Self-Development*. Deerfield Beach, FL: Health Communications, Inc.

Freire, P. (1973) *Pedagogy of the Oppressed*. New York: Continuum.

Fox, J. (1994) *Acts of Service*. New Platz, New York: Tusltala.

Haedeicke, S. and Nellhaus, T. (2001) *Performing Democracy: International Perspectives on Urban Community-Based Performance*. Ann Arbor, MI: University of Michigan Press.

Justice, T. and Jamieson, D.W. (1999) *The Facilitator's Fieldbook*. New York: Amacom.

Katz, N. and Lawyer, J. (1992) *Communication and Conflict Resolution Skills.* Dubuque, IA: Kendall/Hunt Publishing Company.

Kolb, D. (1983) *Experiential Learning: Experience as the Source of Learning.* New York: Prentice Hall.

Kuftinec, S. (2005) *Staging America: Cornerstone and Community Based Theatre.* Carbondale, IL: SIU Press.

Linds, W. (2001) *A Journey to Metaxis: Been, Being, Becoming, Imag(in)ing.* Doctoral Dissertation, University of British Columbia.

Rohd, M. (1998) *Theatre for Community, Conflict, and Dialogue: The Hope is Vital Training Manual.* Portsmouth, NH: Heinemann.

Schutzman, M. and Cohen Cruz, J. (eds) (1994) *Playing Boal: Theatre, Therapy, and Activism.* New York: Routledge.

Schwarz, R. (2002) *The Skilled Facilitator.* San Francisco: Jossey-Bass.

Spolin, V. (1963) *Improvisation for the Theater.* Evanston, IL: Northwestern University Press.

Spolin, V. (1986) *Theater Games for the Classroom: A Teacher's Handbook.* Evanston, IL: Northwestern University Press.

Sternberg, P. (1998) *Theatre for Conflict Resolution: In the Classroom and Beyond.* Portsmouth, NH: Heinemann.

Stringer, E. (1999) *Action Research.* London: Sage.

Van Erven, E. (2001) *Community Theatre: Global Perspectives.* New York: Routledge.

Weigler, W. (2001) *Strategies for Playbuilding: Helping Groups Translate Issues into Theatre.* Portsmouth, NH: Heinemann.

Index